COMMON SENSE
AND
FOREIGN POLICY

JOHN D. STEMPEL

Lexington, Kentucky

For information, address The Clark Group, 250 East Short Street, Lexington, KY 40507. 800-944-3995 | www.theclarkgroupinfo.com | info@theclarkgroupinfo.com

ISBN: 978-1-883589-99-8

Book & cover design by Kelly Elliott

This book is dedicated to
Susan H. Stempel—*mate and muse*
Amy, Alix, and Jill—*our children who lived it with us*
Noah, Olivia, Seth *and any other grandchildren yet to come.*

ACKNOWLEDGEMENTS

As my very good Indian friends would say, a large "vote of thanks" to those who helped with this book, knowingly or not. To my colleagues, friends, and students at the University of Kentucky's Patterson School of Diplomacy and International Commerce. To a generation of terrific Foreign Service Colleagues. To Col. (ret) Pat Mayerchak and his colleagues at Virginia Military Institute, who funded a Spring 2005 sabbatical as the Mary Moody Northen Chair professorship to jump-start the research for the book. To Stephen Wrinn, head of the University Press of Kentucky, whose wisdom and confidence were vital. To Bobby Clark, Florence Huffman, Jennifer Kash, Kelly Elliott, Mark Reinhardt, and the other wizards at The Clark Group, whose motto is "Get it done NOW." Finally, to four-time U.S. Cabinet Officer Elliot Richardson who introduced me to the world of high-level diplomacy.

John D. Stempel
August 2008

CONTENTS

INTRODUCTION

Why buy this book? What does it offer that others don't? After nearly half a century of working in the world of international politics and foreign relations in three different arenas, I bring three perspectives to bear on the question of how to understand foreign policy and participate effectively to improve the public decisions that will determine how we shall live with the rest of the world. Whether you are a citizen, an aspiring participant in foreign affairs, or a jaded veteran of wars and peacekeeping, this book will help you understand the complexities of the subject and stimulate you to get useful information and increase your cross-cultural understanding—both critical areas in which we Americans under-perform.

This should be true regardless of your political views. There is plenty of room for all to do better. Conservatives, moderates and liberals all have something to learn and to contribute about handling foreign issues, but purely partisan, particularly ideological, methods are a substantial part of the problem, especially in international affairs. When people ask about my own views (often with an accusatory "Are you an X or a Y?"), I respond that I am a "Radical Moderate," a label my former boss, four-time U.S. cabinet officer Eliot Richardson, gave himself, and which seems to leave people with a smile and a sense that I seek a balanced picture of matters.

Up until the end of World War II, diplomacy was way down on the list of interests for Americans. Former Undersecretary of State David Newsom writing in *Diplomacy and the American Democracy* put it succinctly:

> The American view of diplomacy is a mixture of ignorance of its details, suspicion of its objectives, contempt for its importance and fascination with its romance.[1]

That changed as America moved into a more active role in world affairs, but not as much as one might hope. I, like many of my generation, read of wars in Korea, became interested and studied foreign affairs, and fought briefly in Vietnam

As a serving military officer in the U.S. Navy in Vietnam and later a civilian director of the Secretary of Defense's Office of Near Eastern and South Asian affairs at the Pentagon, I was part of the military culture and policy process. As a Career Foreign Service Officer for twenty-three years, I was immersed in the Foreign Service culture, serving in developing countries (Guinea, Burundi, Zambia); a country in revolution (Iran—before, during and after the 1979 revolution); an emerging superpower (India). I also had several jobs in Washington, including two years as director the State Department's Operations Center, which helps manage world crises—from hostage takings to major policy problems.

After a three-year tour as Consul General in Madras, India, I retired from the Foreign Service in 1988 to become professor and assistant director—then in 1993 director—of the University of Kentucky's Patterson School of Diplomacy and International Commerce. During that time, and especially since my final stint as director ended in December 2004, I have been working to bring together thoughts and insights about international engagement. In effect, I want to marry the experience of the professor (remain

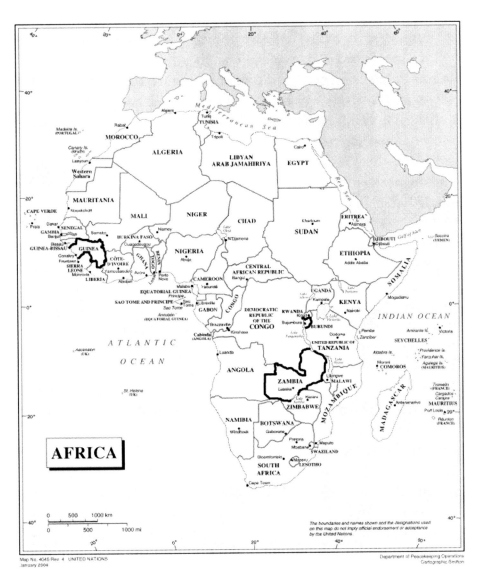

*John Stempel served as a Foreign Service Officer in the three countries with
a heavy dark border.*

objective) with the naval officer-diplomat (seek the facts) and apply that experience to current problems by way of some suggestions on why and how we might improve our national foreign relations.

"Common sense" has many meanings. In this instance, it refers to broad, balanced consideration of as much reliable information as we can absorb, then using it to make solid judgments. It requires a strong knowledge component—being substantially aware of our international environment, our own values, differences with other cultures (which have become much more critical in recent years), and the problems of our own policy processes. There is no magic, single bullet that will improve judgments in our policy/decision making, but there are some things we can do better and some things we should stop doing that will give us a greater measure of common sense, judgment and effectiveness in the future.

While writing this book I would tell people that the working title was "Common Sense and Foreign Policy." The two most common reactions were: "That's an oxymoron, impossible!" and "Short book, huh?" To the contrary, I firmly believe it is possible to understand basic foreign relations, and that our nation's future *depends* upon an informed citizenry. As for "short book," yes it is, but not for the reasons my respondents feared. My objective is to "cut the crap," as my father, veteran newspaperman and journalism professor, told his editing classes for thirty years. This is not an academic study, though some serious academic thought propels it. The footnotes give additional suggestions if the reader wants to pursue a given topic or problem in greater depth; they are not exhaustive.

The current world situation requires us to do certain things much more effectively if we are to cope successfully with, and make good judgments about, our globalizing environment. First, we need to gain more and better knowledge and spread it more widely, about how the world operates, especially about places now unfamiliar to us but increasingly important—the Northwest province of Pakistan, economic and health conditions in Africa, etc. Second, as a people, we need to get inside others' heads to understand how they think and feel—how different cultures "read" the world. This has to be felt and experienced as well as read about. Many young people are increasingly doing this through study and travel abroad. Even more should do so.

If we do these two things, it will be easier to do the rest—press those in public life to do the hard political work of developing policies that actively and effectively cope with both new and old problems. We can do this by unlearning some bad habits, clearing bureaucratic impediments and getting back to the intellectual approaches that have proved most successful in our foreign relations.

Over the past eight years, we have confused the idea of American primacy, a condition, with a policy to aggressively pursue that primacy unilaterally in many areas, notably the invasion of Iraq. The world recognizes that America is the most powerful country in the world—at least for now. Many, if not most, countries accept that fact and are generally willing to work with us. What they do not like, and will not accept, is our insistence that primacy entitles us to have our own way about nearly everything. We appear almost unconscious of how this misapplication of "primacy" has negatively changed others' attitudes toward our country and hindered our own objectives. It is the beam in our own eye.

The growing internal conflict over our unilateralism and especially the Iraq war has resembled ideological bickering rather than a reasoned approach to sorting out our problems. This has adversely affected our decisions and strategies. Working from hard ideological postures means that we deduce our policies from *a priori* positions without sufficient regard for the complexities and nuances of situations on the ground in the "real world." This tends to generate opposition, not acceptance.

Historically, and particularly in the post-World War II period, America has been noted for its pragmatism—we look at cases and take appropriate action to resolve particular problems based on existing conditions and a sober assessment of our capabilities. We have until recently emphasized international cooperation that magnified our influence substantially. Intellectually, this is inductive rather than deductive reasoning and is consistent with common sense and good judgment because it encourages a comprehensive look at events, people and situations, not just intellectual ideas.

My own experience and that of many others suggests that inductive reasoning—looking at situations, first exploring and discussing the beliefs of people involved, then examining the limits and possibilities—is a much better way to conduct foreign relations. Instead of forcing our ideals and values on others regardless of conditions, we should examine the situation and develop policies that help them achieve their goals in harmony with rather than at cross purposes with others. Facing a negative situation one selects policies that minimize damage and impede aggressors whether they are countries or terrorists. In either instance, we have to manage relations with both friends and opponents in a give-and-take process. This requires leadership, not unilateral issuance of commands. When we have led interactively, we have had many followers; when unilaterally, few.

This book examines selected elements of our foreign relations in terms of how expanding our knowledge and cultural understanding of the world can teach us to make more informed judgments and thus be more effective in the world and minimize our danger from it. That is the common sense solution we all seek, but it is neither easy nor even possible unless we work at it in an intelligent, informed manner. Our goal should be to build solid relations with as many like-minded friends as possible. We should also maintain contact with those who oppose us to protect our flanks and gather information; and perhaps ultimately move them out of the opposition camp into alliance, or defeat them militarily if forced to do so.

John D. Stempel
Lexington, Kentucky

---

[1] Newsom, David D. *Diplomacy and the American Democracy.* (Bloomington: Indiana University Press, 2005), p. 6

CHAPTER 1
COMMON SENSE, JUDGMENT & KNOWLEDGE

... within a year or two, the facts break apart ... and slowly began to shift and turn ... until their shapes have been changed and the past has become a new world.

— Ted Kooser, U. S. Poet Laureate, from "Techtonics"

Know or listen to those who know.

—Balthazar Gracian

AT THE ROOT OF COMMON SENSE IS THE ACQUISITION of knowledge and information about life to enable one to render informed judgments on situations or problems. The biggest problem is where to begin, and in what direction to go. In the case of contemporary foreign affairs, the public dialog has been so fraught with struggle and conflict in recent years that it is hard to get a broad, useful picture. We begin with a description of our current international situation and some of the difficulties in maintaining balance and general understanding.

For nearly sixty years until the destruction of the World Trade Center on September 11, 2001, the broad outlines of American foreign policy were easy to understand and explain: fight communism, manage the world economy to increase prosperity, help poorer countries develop, and help democracy grow where possible. While there was always argument over individual goals, our overall objectives were generally balanced enough to achieve substantial agreement that both U.S. political parties could build upon with some degree of cooperation. In support of this, information flowed from the media and professionals to the public, which maintained a reasonable understanding of events.

Even in the years 1966-75, when the war in Vietnam created great divisiveness, both electorate and policy makers returned to moderate, balanced positions that drew positive support from a sizable majority of the country's citizens. As a consequence of the attack on the World Trade Center on September 11, 2001 and subsequent events in its aftermath—especially our invasion of Iraq—the country has been radically split. When this happens in any country, foreign policy suffers.

Over the past four years, when I have been speaking to audiences on various foreign affairs issues, people have asked, "All this seems so complicated—how do you figure out the Iraq problem (or the North Korean nuclear problem, China's expansion, Islamic terrorism, etc.)?" I suggest that they need to get information about the issues and the events. They also need to sort our their own feelings and values since effective foreign policy is based on our basic beliefs, which include our will and capacity to act. What *do* we want to do? Next, assess how we are doing what we are doing—or might do what we propose to do. Should we be doing something different? Do we in fact have the capacity to do it? Do we want to devote the resources to do it? This is an interactive process that continues, sometimes with greater and sometimes lesser focus on international affairs. Just to make it difficult, of course, occasionally leaders and issue proponents don't want to answer such questions, or are mistaken in their answers.

Many then say "What you say sounds like common sense to me." In most cases, it is *informed* common sense (not to be confused with "conventional wisdom," which is what most people believe *without* carefully thinking it through). Such informed common sense, however, requires work—developing a base of factual knowledge, seeking to understand different cultures and their beliefs. Sometimes—as in the recent past—there is hardly enough agreement to even have a widely accepted conventional wisdom at this point in our national debate, and we are left to sort out a conundrum.

Public dialog becomes difficult. People with firm ideological views propose ideas that many suspect will not work in practice. On some important points, the government persists in error to the point of folly (Chapter 3), yet its critics have not yet carried the day. Our professionals—diplomats, and intelligence and military officers—are asked to take actions they strongly suspect will fail, and those higher up at the political level refuse to listen to constructive feedback, "reality checks," which do not fit their ideological perceptions. Over the past five years, our reputation has been severely damaged both here and abroad—because our sense of being a superpower, or "empire," has endowed too many in public life with a sense of arrogance and entitlement. It has made them forgetful of some basic truths of human nature as well as disdainful of cultures they do not understand. More about this in chapters 2 and 3.

There are four basic reasons for this sorry state of our foreign relations and politics:

First, foreign affairs have always been something of a mystery. The structure of the international system has changed, and the amount of knowledge required to understand it has expanded greatly since the end of the Cold War. Places that seemed irrelevant then—such as Kosovo, Rwanda and Darfur—suddenly become major problems at a time when we are focused elsewhere. Our educational system is struggling to catch up with our information and conceptual needs. Perhaps just as important, the majority of people do not have time to follow more than a few issues at a time, if they follow foreign affairs at all. As a large continental-size country, we are less aware of the different cultures and cultural issues that have become much more important in the past eighteen years. Even though we have become more diverse ourselves in the past twenty years, this has not yet been significantly reflected in our international dealings.

— Second, as problems become more complex and less focused on one or two issues, clear choices become difficult, and questions of values—what we should do rather than what we must do—have become more important. As America has become the "sole remaining superpower," and is clearly recognized as the most powerful single country in the world (at least for now), we have greater freedom to act for both good and ill—but that's still less than many of us have assumed. When the U.S. was focused on the Cold War, nearly all issues were defined and actions advocated on the basis of how they would advance our interests in that bipolar struggle with an adversary that wielded great power. Today there are many divergent views of the national interest that are difficult to know and even more difficult to assess. There are more options and more freedom, but this can often be confusing as well as liberating.

— Third, the complexity of modern society and the tendency toward greater specialization has made it harder to use common sense. People—political and foreign policy elites as well as ordinary citizens—become linked to particular institutions or systems of thought that discourage the kind of overall assessment that both sound strategy and common sense demand. Bureaucratic aspects of making policy in a complex age mean that both individuals and organizations have more difficulty pulling everything together in a consensus view of the national interest, or even agreeing on the values we should be advocating. Organizational communication is severely crimped when the difference between belief and knowledge at different levels is deep.

— Fourth, politics in the U.S. has become more divisive and symbolic in the past thirty years than the thirty that preceded them. The country pays a price—it is much more difficult to weigh various points of view, the need for argument drives one to extremes, and the American freedom of choice and primacy of power encourages arrogance and ideological mindsets. In thinking ourselves unilaterally powerful, we forget that a principal component of that power in the recent past has been our highly positive relationships with other countries, allies and friends. When we now try to boss others around and force them to do our bidding, we encounter resistance and drag. The attitude of our traditional allies toward the 2003 Iraq War is an excellent example—their refusal to help in a serious way stands in stark contrast to their financial support that paid for the first Gulf War in 1990-91 in the first President Bush's administration.

So now we have to know more about more arcane things and places—the AIDS pandemic and Uzbekistan, for example—than we did before. This makes sorting out values and determining how the country should act more complicated since the 9/11 attack, neoconservatives both in and out of government, and since 2002 the Bush administration, assert that "American primacy" means we can and should act alone without paying much heed to other countries. They extol the use of force rather than diplomacy and disdain our sixty-year tradition of working closely with other countries. We pay a heavy price for this sort of arrogance.

Others, both at home and abroad, from more cooperative traditions, call upon us to build stronger communities with others—both nation-to-nation and people-to-people, through public diplomacy as well as privately with non-government groups. To do this, however, both leaders and citizens must relearn the value of public diplomacy and how to build effective relationships for action. An overwhelming number of scholars and diplomats emphasize that this takes reciprocal concern for other people rather than simply imposing one's way.[1]

Whom do we listen to, and how do we sort out expert from charlatan or ideologue and apply "common sense" to problems? Our political system has not done a particularly commendable job in helping us to sort out alternatives since the destruction of the Twin Towers on September 11, 2001. The nongovernmental establishment has produced studies, but these are mostly for specialists. Those within government who have suggested better ways to proceed have been pushed to the margins, or forced out like former Secretary of State Colin Powell. How should we approach these issues so we *can* bring good judgment and hence "common sense" to bear on foreign affairs?

First, expand our knowledge. As a society, we need more and better education—but it has to be self-education for those no longer in school. It's harder to grasp the basic principles of international relations enough to be sufficiently informed now than it was twenty years ago. In 1945, the United Nations consisted of fifty member states. The end of colonialism and other political developments increased UN membership to 192 at present. Areas that were quiescent decades ago, such as Central Asia, are now central to resource struggles (oil) and Islamic politics.

Globalization—the continued integration of all economies on a global basis—has changed the way we think about traditional issues of foreign trade, domestic employment and financial balance. U.S. trade deficits have reached record proportions, jobs have been exported abroad, and China now holds a disproportionate share of our foreign debt.

Religion has reentered politics both domestically and abroad. This began during and after World War II. The creation of the state of Israel in 1948 brought to the international political stage an Islamic renaissance that began in the late nineteenth century and gathered steam after Jewish immigration to Palestine increased substantially after World War I. This was capped by the later emergence of terrorism as a political force, and more recently the emergence of Al Qaeda, a non-national terrorist organization based on a very fundamentalist form of Islamic ideology. This has become a major threat to personal as well as national security. More about this in chapters 4 and 5.

Remember, however, that historically religion has also been the root of our own views on foreign affairs since the country was founded. This hasn't been specifically in a policy sense, but through an overall belief in God and the general feeling that America was a special nation under Divine providence.

Political parties had different approaches of course, but certainly from the end of World War II until the middle of the Vietnam War—about 1968—there was general agreement on what we should do and even what most of the alternatives were. With the Vietnam trauma ended by our departure from Saigon in 1975, Democrats began to be less enthusiastic about building military alliances abroad; by 1980 the Republicans were pushing for greater strength in the armed services. A military buildup followed in the first few years of the Reagan administration, followed by a slight reduction under the first President Bush, and a greater one under President Clinton. Military expenditure has grown under the current president, but mostly in connection with the invasion of Iraq in 2003. Estimates suggest the effort in Iraq will end up costing in excess of $1.6 trillion.

Economically, the U.S. went off the gold standard in 1971, but the dollar remained the major world currency because of U.S. economic strength. The U.S. worked through the multilateral financial institutions—The World Bank and the International Monetary Fund— and private banking systems to control adverse fluctuations. It is now much more difficult to do so with the rising economic power of both China and India affecting the world stage. Some even see the end of American primacy in half a century's time.

President William "Bill" Jefferson Clinton
Source:
www.defenseimagery.mil

Post-World War II policy judgment and common sense suggested that we cooperate with allies and others to preserve peace and boost the world economy. Western Europe achieved substantial unity and Japan became an important economic partner. Thoughtful histories of American foreign policy and international relations show a relatively coherent view of international relations, despite the occasional crisis.[2]

Certain problems marred the general consensus. The birth of Israel began a struggle in the Middle East between Arabs and Israel, which has evolved over 60 years in such a way that it thrust religion back into international relations and diplomacy. This reversed a 350-year long process by which religion had been essentially separated from diplomacy after the Treaty of Westphalia in 1648.

In the early 1970s, Europe beat back serious terrorist threats by several nationally organized groups. The U.S. and the Soviet Union each suffered from interventions in small countries (Vietnam, Afghanistan), which demonstrated that there were actually limits to superpowerhood. The general outlines of the international system, however, remained fairly firmly in place until 1989.

The "post-Cold War" era began with the demise of the Soviet Union in 1989-1991 and the reunion of East and West Germany. Over the next fifteen years a number of changes altered the way we look at the world. The most significant was that the United States became the "sole remaining superpower." The Soviet Union broke up into Russia and fifteen other associated states, and Russian power diminished dramatically through the economic and political collapse of the Soviet "empire." Other aspirants to "superpowerhood"—China and India are the most mentioned—sped up their economic growth.

These two countries' rapidly growing need for energy is currently increasing the pressure on resources, reflected notably on oil, driving the price to new heights. India and China are several decades away from posing a serious military challenge to the U.S., even if they wanted to do so, and indeed war between major powers is deemed highly unlikely.[3] Nevertheless, these countries will play very important roles in international relations over the next fifty years, creating both problems and opportunities, especially in the economic realm. These relationships will certainly not be amenable to American-dictated policies and will require careful diplomatic tending.

A whole new range of problems has been stimulated by the rise of Islamic terrorism and its accelerated growth after the September 11, 2001 destruction of the World Trade Center. The U.S. and Pakistan built up the Taliban in the 1980s to help force the Soviet Union out of Afghanistan. After the Russian departure from Afghanistan in 1989, the U.S. withdrew from the region and neglected it for more than a decade until 9/11. The Taliban slowly took over Afghanistan, and the result was the substantial growth of Al Qaeda and increasing terrorist incidents in the 1990s. The U.S. and most other Western countries severely lagged in understanding this phenomenon until 9/11, despite the earlier experiences.

Since September 2001, significant differences emerged both internationally and domestically on how the international system is supposed to deal with other important issues. President Bush, instead of completing the destruction of the Taliban after his initial foray into Afghanistan, redirected the American effort toward the invasion of Iraq in March 2003. He did this despite severe differences with key allies Germany and France, and major discord within his own administration over the seriousness of the Iraqi security threat to the U.S. and that country's relationship to Islamic terrorism. Additionally, since the year 2000, American refusal to join the International Criminal Court, to sign the Kyoto treaty on global warming and to work closely with the UN have pushed us away from America's traditional post-World War II willingness to work in cooperation with others. To others, including allies, such actions and positions raise questions abroad about our future intentions, as well as creating resistance to our wishes on such issues as sending troops to help in Iraq. In sum, we have tried to impose unilateral deductive solutions without proper attention to relationships. It doesn't work.

Second, examine our values and how we express them—and learn why/how others see them differently. The U.S. is overdue for a major sorting out of who we are and where we want to go. The changed international environment and subsequent adaptation of a "politics of primacy" by the Bush administration, including its adoption of preventive and preemptive war doctrine, thrust the issue of values to the forefront. Preemptive war to ward off imminent and dangerous threat has always been recognized as a last resort, but preventive war to stop another power from acquiring certain capabilities—Iran and nuclear weapons, for example—smacks of aggression to many, including our allies.[4] "Preemptive war" has been the excuse for most aggressors in history, and that is how some now see us.

Colin Powell, former Secretary of State, NSTAC XXVII Meeting, May 2004
Source: National Communications System

9/11 caused everyone to think "outside the box" about terrorism. In America, the dominance of the neoconservatives within the Bush administration coupled with the change from Colin Powell to Condoleezza Rice as secretary of state in 2005 signaled clear administration preference for a go-it-alone policy for the U.S. after its inability to get major allies to agree with the necessity to invade Iraq two years earlier. Both the "go-it-alone" view, and the Iraq War have raised questions at home and abroad as to whether "primacy as policy" serves American interests well, and if not, what American values ought to apply and how should they be expressed.[5]

The 2004 presidential election highlighted the deep division within America—as deep as any since Vietnam, or even the 1940-41 pre-World War II isolationist era. This has significantly increased the difficulty of conducting foreign policy, and at the same time brings ideology strongly into questions of judgment. This inhibits applying

Condoleezza Rice, Secretary of State
Source: Wikipedia, Department of State

common sense—since there are now at least two or three versions of "common sense" running around the political arena: enthusiastically pro-Bush who want to go-it-alone; equally fervent anti-Bush who value cooperation; a growing group of those who are undecided and unsure but are unhappy with partisan extremes; plus a few exemplified by the Missouri woman who answered a pollster's query, "I never vote—it only encourages the damn fools."

Once values come into play, religion comes along as well. This, coupled with religious extremism and terrorism abroad and more active religious fundamentalism at home, opens debates about our bedrock ends and means and the methods used to achieve them. It brings religious questions back

Detainees in jumpsuits sit in a holding area under the watchful eyes of Military Police at Camp X-Ray at Naval Base Guantanamo Bay, Cuba, during in-processing to the temporary detention facility on Jan. 11, 2002.
Source: Wikipedia, photo by Shane T. McCoy, U.S. Navy

into politics. The intense discussion over the Abu Ghraib prison scandals in Iraq and military interrogations at the Guantanamo holding facility raise both legal and moral questions of who is a legitimate prisoner of war, how extensive should interrogations be, and what the trade-offs between security and morality become.

The result is deeper and more fundamental disagreements over the principles of conduct in foreign affairs, and how these apply to judgment on current policy issues. In our democracy this significantly slows development of a policy consensus, thwarts consistent planning and use of resources, and reduces public support for policies that emerge. An unfortunate cause *and* by-product of this situation is government's increasing disinclination to listen to criticism and alternative ideas, which tends to preclude development of effective, supportable policies. It is not easy to inject common sense and judgment into this mix—but it will be essential for national survival.

Third, attack the problem of obtaining unbiased and reliable information. The body politics need to insist on an end to such practices as doctoring intelligence to fit, such as occurred with the question of Iraq's weapons of mass destruction (WMDs).[6] Deep differences over policy and values complicate both layman's and expert's ability to sort out fact from rhetoric. This is historically true as well. Psychology tells us that people's beliefs color their views of a given situation, and lead them to discard or downplay information that challenges their views. Hence, the rigidity of an ideological position produces an equally fervent challenge, substantially narrowing the potential area of reasonable agreement.

Many doubtless react to such news with the same ironic tone Claude Rains took in *Casablanca* while standing in a gambling casino collecting his winnings: "I'm shocked, *shocked*, I tell you, to hear that gambling is taking place here." The strong Bush supporter sees only progress from the insurgency statistics out of Iraq; his anti-Bush counterpart cites the same statistics as evidence that the insurgency is spreading. Neither has much time to sympathize with the academic or citizen who want to get the bluster out of the problem and wants hard evidence he or she can absorb.

The same pressures also affect research institutions with liberal or conservative bents and reputations. Here one can find researchers either dealing with issues that lead to "good" results, or working on certain problems rather than others because they are directed to study them. Especially in an intensely conflictual situation, findings that challenge orthodoxy are more quietly shelved instead of serving as a point of discussion. These tendencies are not extensive, but they underline a point: One must seek out critical reasoning and not limit oneself to viewpoints with blinders. This also means working a little harder at acquiring accurate knowledge.

Academics and media face the same kinds of pressures. Media folk are, by the nature of their profession, looking for a story (some critics occasionally say they're trying to generate a problem: "Let's you and him fight!") They can easily become caught up in differences of opinion as well because controversies are often what make news. America has woefully fewer in-depth journalistic analysts than it needs, especially for places like the Middle East and Central Asia. The fragmentation of the electronic media, with many more news sources since the 1970s, also inhibits building consensus, as fewer watch the major network national news programs.

Some academics also nearly take themselves out of the policy process. They produce quantitative research that rarely approaches utility for dealing with policy questions. This leads to a tendency to try to reduce politics, and hence the discipline of political science, to quantitative findings and to downplay information other than mathematical. This can leave vital information off the table, and

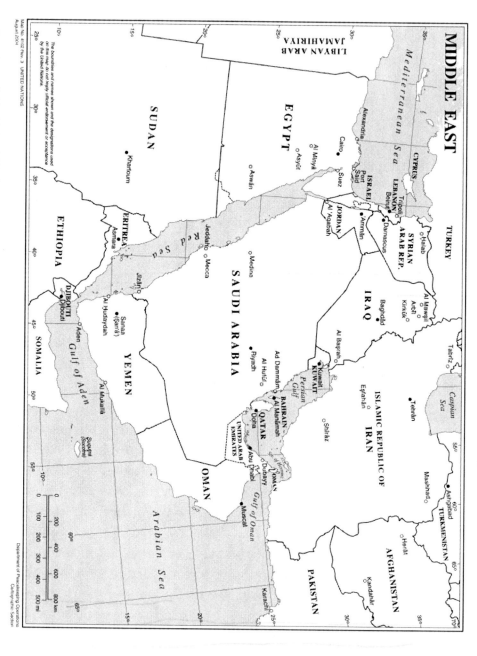

MIDDLE EAST

Map No. 4102 Rev. 3 UNITED NATIONS
August 2004

The boundaries and names shown and the designations used
on this map do not imply official endorsement or acceptance
by the United Nations.

Department of Peacekeeping Operations
Cartographic Section

Courtesy of the United Nations

gives people very little help on value choices that are not quantifiable. Quantitative studies are a particularly poor way of studying the critical intangibles of other cultures and subtler diplomatic efforts that do not lend themselves well to numerical estimates.[7]

Many scholars do work to develop policy-relevant knowledge, but as astute and well-respected political scientist Alexander George has noted, analysis itself can be an aid to judgment, but even the highest quality analysis can only aid in making a decision. It is not a substitute for the comprehensive judgment of a policy-maker. Analysis can narrow the workable options and point in certain directions, but it may have little impact on other key factors such as timing, scope and objective.[8]

There is no more a "magic bullet" for reaching a common sense perspective, than for making a solidly researched decision. On the other hand, the more a broad common sense view encompasses better and more information and concern for values, the better and more accurate judgment is likely to be. Two examples make the point:

1. President Bush's decision to ignore allied opinion in going to war with Iraq in 2003 can be criticized because it dismisses or ignores those we need to help us.

2. In the spring of 2006, the Bush administration reaffirmed its decision to use the National Guard both abroad; and on the U.S. southern border to stem illegal immigration. Some military analysts said this would downgrade the guard's capabilities; the administration denied it vehemently. Most average citizens could (and many did) learn the truth by asking their friends and neighbors in the guard if they were going to re-enlist. The results were overwhelmingly negative, and are beginning to show—the guard will rapidly loose trained cadres over the next two or three years, with important implications for national security as well as for homeland disaster relief.

When the total number of unexamined and unintended negative consequences adds up, even stubbornness (a fine quality in certain instances) will not save the day.

Fourth, move away from divisive politics and seek foreign policy consensus. American history is clear on one point: Foreign affairs work better when backed by a broad coalition with fundamental agreement on value issues. Some politicians strive to divide, while others want to build inclusive coalitions. When politics becomes as vitriolic as it has over the past four years, experts, pundits and politicians get caught up in the argument of the day. Those in government cannot admit a mistake, and those opposed can see nothing but error.

It has happened before—Korea, 1952-53 and Vietnam, 1966-75 are examples. The debate over the Iraq war dwarfs them both because it deals with more fundamental issues with further impact—the specter of continuing and expanding future terrorism. Controversy develops into a question of whether winning an argument rather than a keen assessment and judgment is best for the national interest. Emotion begins to dominate intellect, and logical argument gets lost.[9] This process often is aided and abetted by journalists and TV commentators, who focus more on the immediate than on the important, and by the networks, who give increasingly less time to international stories.

Our failure to study history and the deeper implications of what we are doing causes us as a nation to loose track of the strategic picture. For example, in 2003 the U.S. Army found itself facing a guerrilla insurgency in Iraq that Pentagon civilian planners denied would happen. Yet despite its experiences in Vietnam just thirty years earlier, there has been little training—except for a few small Special Forces groups. New operations manuals had to be pasted together from 1970s material found in U.S. Special Forces warehouses. With a little additional editing and updating, a new manual was finally published in 2007.[10] Time and lives were wasted.

The real nature of problems becomes lost in symbolic language. Senior political leaders pay scant attention to active commanders and diplomats. Reality is poorly understood at the top; leaders under pressure become increasingly arrogant and less open, and the public gets a skewed view of what is really going on. People cling tenaciously to positions that become questionable at best, and common sense and judgment gives way to less rational political combat.

Such behavior can be found in any arena where there are profound differences. Some call it a loss of civility, but it is often more destructive than that—warping, twisting or stopping discussion. Logical argument falls by the wayside while people cleave to various mantras and symbols. This is frequently true of political arguments, and those about international affairs are no exception.

BUILDING KNOWLEDGE, APPLYING JUDGMENT

There is much we can do and several things to keep in mind to build knowledge successfully and apply good judgment with balanced and informed judgment. Doing so will counter the pressures against common sense described above. Seeking good sources for information, staying aware of the problems, and looking for the rigidities in both individuals and bureaucracies is a good start. Seeking a broad view of problems and identifying rigid ideological positions should be another effort. Sometimes Folk wisdom and common sense are effective in loosening dialog and gaining a broader perspective for judgment. Individuals and institutions *can* act to increase the prospect that flawed solutions can be avoided.

Of course, people begin from different levels of information and education, different values, different desires, and varying openness to new ideas and information. Medical doctors are experts in surgery and treatment, but know little about building and using rockets. Foreign affairs specialists, at least until relatively recently, knew much about the use of force and statecraft, but little about the growing impact of religion on contemporary foreign policy. Few would try to tell a surgeon how to perform an operation because they have not had surgical training, but too many believe they should direct our foreign policy even though they have had neither relevant training or experience.

The growing bureaucratization of modern society in the past 140 years has led to rigidities and organizational points of view that help clarify but also occasionally help distort perceptions. A thoughtful example is the story of Admiral William "Bull" Halsey's wife, at a large dinner party with all the top American military officers at Pearl Harbor on the evening of December 6, 1941. Discussion concentrated on the impending Japanese attack—where would it take place? Australia? Indochina? Commanders gave measured views based on current doctrine. Mrs. Halsey, speaking from intuition and curiosity, startled the group by asking: "But what if they attack here, at Pearl Harbor?" Everyone present assured her this could not happen, and chuckled about her lack of military knowledge. Almost exactly twelve hours later the bombs began falling.[11]

Except for a few terrorist experts, on September 10, 2001, one could have gotten the same dismissive response to suggestions about using commercial airline flights to destroy the World Trade Center. One of the most important components we should all have in our endeavors is to seek out information and be appropriately humble about what we consider to be certainties.

Everyone begins from assumptions about how things "work." Our reasoning is based on information and evidence, concepts and ideas. Our conclusions have implications and consequences. Whenever we approach a problem, we need to fully understand our assumptions and seek out relevant information. This is particularly true about issues involving matters on which we have little personal experience. We may know a great deal about pricing new cars or rewiring our basement, but not so much on the larger and broader issues of war and peace. We may not even be sure where to look, or even how much time we want to spend looking up information. Some methods and sources are discussed more thoroughly in chapter 8.

But that's not all—if getting information and thinking about it were all that is required to develop wise and well-prepared foreign policy, the world wouldn't be where it is today. In addition to questions of knowledge, insight, will, and the need to build an organized coalition around successful policies, we need to find ways around certain impediments that can thwart the best intentions.

Overcoming Impediments to Judgment

The principal deficit in American understanding about the rest of the world is lack of knowledge of other cultures and specifically what other cultures think about us. Our press and media generally do not do a good enough job of reflecting foreign attitudes, particularly those expressing underlying negative beliefs about America. Also, Americans are not terribly attentive to negative feedback until something dramatic occurs—Pearl Harbor, 9/11, etc. Our focus on "primacy" as "telling others what to do" has exacerbated these attitudes and pushed us towards abandoning our historic pragmatics and deductive policy/decision-making.

Over several years this has led to an inadequate understanding of the negative shift in opinion about the U.S. and its government. Since the 2003 invasion of Iraq, favorable foreign public views of the U.S. have dropped from well above fifty percent to mid-thirty percent. In the Middle East, approval of the U.S. has been in single digits or below twenty percent during the 2003-2005 period, then rising before returning to its lowest level in the summer of 2006, after the Israeli bombings in Lebanon.[12] Perhaps the most dangerous aspect of this is that even top politicians and experts too often display such cultural insensitivity.

A related impediment is the problem of trying to sort out the implications—costs, benefits, etc.—of measures proposed, especially when there are strong differences on what needs to be done. American views on broad questions of war and peace, humanitarian aid, and economic measures to cope with globalization, are often vague and subject to battering from all sides. This is particularly true in the current period of strong disagreement about the invasion of Iraq, treatment of prisoners, government spending on foreign affairs, and immigration.

The ideological tone that has crept into public discussion of foreign affairs has increased susceptibility to both of the problems noted above. This tone increases the difficulty in getting accurate projections. It is reinforced by a bureaucratic structure of government that tends to be hostile to dissenting opinions—hence bureaucratic self-corrective efforts to avoid mistakes are generally more often suppressed than exploited by organizational leaders, at least unless and until a disaster occurs.

Right-wing attacks on the State Department and efforts to suppress unpleasant findings offer a sad example. Such attacks contributed significantly to the situation where a well-researched department task force report on the future of Iraq that took two years to prepare was ignored in the preparations for the 2003 invasion of the country. Further, talented Arab-speaking Foreign Service officers who worked on the report were barred from serving with the first coalition authority, depriving America of the very expertise it most needed.[13] No one with a shred of judgment or common sense should have accepted this situation. Diplomats should have protested; Congress should have acted; and the public should have been outraged, but it knew too little too late. Little comment was heard.

Actual policies followed also tend over time to become disconnected from broad, sweeping strategic views. Historically, this has often been a pretty good thing since actual events rarely conform to the sweeping visions of the policy planner. In fact, one of the best qualities of American politics has often been its pragmatism— if you're headed for disaster, change course. As Ralph Waldo Emerson put it, "A foolish consistency is the hobgoblin of little minds, adored by little statesmen and philosophers and divines."

Ralph Waldo Emerson, author, essayist, poet (1803-1882)
Source: Wikipedia, drawing by Samuel Worcester Rowse

The operating departments of government in the State and Defense Departments, especially State's regional bureaus (Europe, Africa, Middle East, etc.), have to make policy sense out of sweeping policy pronouncements such as "expand democracy in the Middle East," or "oppose genocide." They also then have to discover and manage the unforeseen consequences of actions undertaken for one purpose that produce another. The President calls for an end to AIDS in Africa, but it is the officers in the African Bureau who have to whip the policy together, badger their bosses for resources, and convince their overseas partner countries.

American values are woven into this process at all levels, but alas, they are often conflicting ones. A desire to increase trade for economic reasons often runs afoul of those who seek to expand fair labor practices. Our belief that the U.S. enjoys "special providence" from the Almighty often clashes with others' view of themselves as distinctive and superior. Some regard war as a necessary evil of the international system, while pacifists abhor all violence. Weaving these elements into a cohesive policy with strong support is never easy and frequently impossible. The historic result has been an alternation between interventionist and isolationist policy-making tendencies throughout our history. Chapter 2 discusses these circumstances.

Common sense and judgment, then, involve acquiring relevant knowledge and establishing a total picture that makes sense and avoids as many impediments as possible. Below are six guides to help do this:

SIX GUIDES TO IMPROVING FOREIGN POLICY

1. Learn what you can about both sides of an issue and the values at stake. Chapter 8, the Bibliography, and the Appendix offer some concrete suggestions and resources. Work on this *before* voicing firm and definitive opinions. Remember the old adage: "It is better to remain silent and be thought a fool than to speak and remove all doubt."

2. Support policies that are in general harmony with your values. Rarely will issues be crystal clear. If they were, they wouldn't be issues. In international affairs, perhaps more than in other aspects of public life, an important reality to keep in mind is that the choice is often not between the bad and the good, but the bad and the horrible. You will never (or only very, very rarely) hear a politician admit this, and then only after he or she leaves office.

3. Seek to find the real present and future costs of policies. Start by looking at both the positive and negative aspects associated with any policy. Listen to professionals more than politicians. Remember: the bigger the task the more it costs—our "quick" adventure in Iraq is heading past $1.6 trillion. Press for details: do not accept "It's too complicated." Be sure to remember Sean Connery's advice to Wesley Snipes in the movie *Rising Sun*: "If something is too good to be true, it probably isn't."

4. Be very suspicious of those who deny the obvious under pressure. Politicians, policy makers and bureaucrats will change their views under political and organizational pressure. No surprise there, we have ample evidence of this even in the intelligence community. It is often amazing how smart people can be led into doing dumb things by pressure.[14]

5. Shun and discount those who are arrogant beyond self-confidence. They will not only err, but convert error into folly and then disaster (see chapter 3). Being smart does not automatically make one wise. Arrogance, egocentrism, omniscience and omnipotence are often diseases of the very intelligent. Arrogance and hubris are currently the most serious impediments to sound American foreign policy. A sense of humility, moderation and balance are critical tools for wise action; all of our best leaders possess at least some of each.

6. Keep in mind that foreign policy always involves others. Will a given approach help or hinder building relationships? Because of our power as a nation we have become accustomed to having our way. This will not long remain the case if we do not pay attention to the values and opinions of those who are not of our tribe. For sixty years we have managed, with a great deal of help and support, an international system which has brought peace in difficult times and prosperity to many. Most of the world wants to join us and wants us to succeed, but they won't continue to do so if we persist in defining our hegemony or "superpowerhood" in terms of doing anything we want to do without concern for at least the tacit goodwill of many, if not most, of those "others." We need to bring them into the game.

Historically, from an organizational view, most historians and scholars regard America as a pragmatic country, not an ideological one. In simple terms, this means that if we try something and it doesn't seem to work, we don't persist in it, but change it. In the few instances, particularly recent ones, when we have not followed this path, we have suffered. We have prospered best when we have had a general, informed consensus on the main elements of our policies built upon interaction with other nations and international actors and responded to them. Humorist Josh Billings once observed, "Common Sense is instinct and enough of it is genius." But excellent instinct is made up of sound knowledge, preparation, experience and judgment.

---

[1] Saunders, Harold. *Politics is About Relationships* (New York: Palgrave Macmillan, 2005), pp. 9-59; and Amitai Etzioni, *From Empire to Community* (New York: Palgrave Macmillan, 2006), pp. 73-94 and 195-214.

[2] Herring, George M. and John C. Carroll. *Modern American Diplomacy* (Wilmington, DE: Scholarly Resources Inc., 1996). ch. 1 and conclusion; and Mingst, Karen. *Essentials of International Relations* (New York: W.W. Norton and Company, 2004), chs. 2-4.

[3] Jervis, Robert. *American Foreign Policy in a New Era* (Routledge, NY: Routledge, 2005), pp. 52-58.

[4] Walt, Stephen. *Taming American Power* (New York: Norton, 2006), pp. 60-61.

[5] Kohut, Andrew and Bruce Stokes. *America Against the World* (New York: Henry Holt and Company, 2006), pp. 22-40.

[6] Risen, James. *State Of War: The Secret History of the CIA and the Bush Administration* (New York: Free Press, 2006), chs. 4 and 6; and Suskind, Ron. *The One Percent Doctrine* (New York: Simon and Schuster, 2006) ch. 1.

[7] Walt, Stephen M. "Rigor or Rigor Mortis? Rational Choice and Security Studies," *International Security 23* (Spring 1999): pp. 5-48; and Chon, Jonathan. "When Did Political Science Forget About Politics? Irrational Exuberance," *The New Republic* (New York), 25 October 1999, pp. 25-32.

[8] George, Alexander. *Bridging the Gap* (Washington: U.S. Institute of Peace, 1998); and George, Alexander. *On Foreign Policy* (Boulder, CO: Paradigm Publishers, 2006).

[9] Lapham, Lewis. *Gag Rule: On the Suppression of Dissent and Stifling of Democracy* (New York: Penguin, 2004).

[10] Nagel, John A. (ed) *U.S. Army Field/Marine Corps Counterinsurgency Manual*, (Washington: U.S. Government Printing Office, 2007).

[11] Janis, Irving L. *Groupthink: Psychological Studies of Policy Decisions and Fiascoes* (New York: Houghton Mifflin Company, 1982), pp. 75-76.

[12] Kohut and Stokes, op cit., pp. 162-92.

[13] Gingrich, Newt. "Rogue State Department," *Foreign Policy* (Washington), July/August 2003, p. 42; and Hirsh, Seymour. "Last Stand," *The New Yorker* (New York), July 10, 2006, pp. 42-49. Suskind, ch. 7-9.

[14] If you don't believe this, please read: Sternberg, Robert J. *Why Smart People Can Be So Stupid* (New Haven, CT: Yale University Press, 2002).

CHAPTER 2
AMERICAN PRIMACY & DIPLOMACY

Things fall apart; The center cannot hold; Mere anarchy is loosed upon the world. The blood-dimmed tide is loosed and everywhere ... The best lack all conviction and the worst are full of passionate intensity.

—W.B. Yeats, *The Second Coming*

SINCE 2002, THE QUESTION OF AMERICAN PRIMACY AND the issue of appropriate American diplomacy have been primary subjects of concerned discussion by everyone connected with American foreign policy—theorists, policy and decision makers, and citizens. All recognize American primacy as a condition, neither good nor bad, which is recognized by most other nations. But those who insist that maintaining primacy by all means possible are endorsing a policy of battling everyone who questions it. They are thus arguing a policy that aggressors have used to justify their conquests for over three thousand years.

American neoconservatives have argued that America is the most powerful nation in the world and therefore can and *should* act unilaterally as it wishes. In doing so, they cross the line from primacy as a condition and make unilateral maintenance of primacy a policy objective. Most traditional American internationalists and others challenge they "therefore can act unilaterally," noting that America has succeeded superbly in the past sixty years by cooperating with others in a combined effort, not by insisting on doing what it wished regardless of others.[1]

The issues of American primacy and the accompanying unilateralist primacy diplomacy of the Bush administration, especially as they have played out over the past six years in the Middle East, have made U.S. foreign policy a major negative focus of national and international concern. Our overall conduct in Iraq played a key role in the 2004 presidential election, the results of which, the President claimed, ratified our Iraqi policy. He asserted that there was no reason to hold any administration officials accountable for mistakes or misjudgments in prewar planning or managing the violent aftermath.[2]

Perhaps President Bush believed his own assertion, but subsequent events brought comparisons with our extended involvement in Vietnam and resulted in a steady and continuing drop in the President's standing in the polls. His overall favorable ratings now stand at twenty-eight percent, with seventy-four percent opposed to going to war merely to combat authoritarianism—just below where Lyndon Johnson stood in 1968 on Vietnam. Common sense and study suggest that the last few years have put the U.S. in an uncomfortable and unfortunate position, but there is no national agreement on either whether this is so, or why. The result has been deep division along and within party lines.

The existence of primacy strongly affects the public view and our basic values and posture as a nation in foreign affairs. How we choose to behave has important implications for our own safety and others' well being. How we relate to the world in the coming decade and beyond will determine our future, but the path is far from clear. Most of our nation's most experienced foreign policy officials and many scholars feel there is considerable danger in a unilateralist posture, and that going to war without stronger international support has been disastrous.

The reality is complex: never has America been so powerful; seldom has it felt so vulnerable. This is the paradox America faces as it deals with crucial questions of war and peace, especially in the Middle East. There, following the invasion of Afghanistan, the military liberation of Iraq has been the centerpiece of the American War on Terror, and in the summer of 2006, the Arab-Israeli clash entered a new phase in Lebanon with unfortunate choices and results. A year later, by the summer of 2007, our position in Afghanistan was deteriorating and under challenge. Rising casualties in Afghanistan were making the administration's position even more difficult.[3]

The events of September 11, 2001 and those that followed—the invasion of Iraq—and deterioration in Afghanistan and Lebanon—transformed America's image of itself and of its role. Until then, the U.S. proudly basked in Francis Fukyama's democratic triumphalism and the victory of American values, including both market economics and liberal political democracy, seemed assured.

There was no great power opposition. The U.S. had won the Cold War, seen by many as the third world war of the twentieth century. Communism had been decisively defeated and discredited. The Soviet Union was no longer either a moral or military power. American military power not only vastly surpassed that of any potential rival, be it Russia or China, but exceeded that of all our traditional allies combined. The American economy was on a roll, the deficit had been eliminated and, American technology and productivity were second to none. Friends and foes alike acknowledged our power. The French went so far as to label us a "hyperpower." Others called us a global hegemon and some European and American scholars were already talking of an American "Empire."[4]

Practically, other governments and international organizations tended toward our way. America was the unquestioned leader of a coalition of freedom-loving peoples. We were not merely first among equals as many thought in the U.S.-Soviet bipolar era after World War II, or in the multi-power imperial world post-World War I. We were the unchallenged number one; triumphalism was the order of the day.[5]

The destruction of the World Trade Center and damage to the Pentagon on 9/11 changed all that and brought about an atmosphere of fear. It was easy to wonder whether our gains were all mere illusion. Our seeming invincibility gave way to a stark realization of how exposed we were to the asymmetrical forces of terrorism—the new terrorism of global reach. Later, when our "shock and awe" victory in Iraq was followed within months by a deadly insurgency, our fears grew even more, as we failed to either prevent or control that growing insurgency.

To understand American policy and our current choices, one must understand how that mindset has played out over the past six years, and what the steps we have taken since then portend for the future.

Many foreign and domestic commentators were quick to assume that Al Qaeda's demonstration of America's vulnerability meant that our primacy was an illusion. Because we had oversold our primacy before 9/11, others began to underestimate our power and our ability to influence the course of events in the new world of fundamentalist Islamic terrorism. The truth is that the U.S. *is* "number one" in most important ways—political, economic, social and military. The *real* question is "What does being number one really mean in terms of exercising military and political power, undertaking successful diplomacy, and controlling our own economic destiny?" There, the answers are much less clear. Dominance does not mean all-powerfulness. Our natural allies in Europe and Asia now question our leadership and our resources have proved all too finite as we contemplate the next several years and the mounting challenges in the Middle East and Central Asia.

The most difficult question is whether American primacy is sufficient to excuse the nation from the historical pressures on empires and powerful states, as historians and others have pointed out.[6] Specifically, does our current preeminence permit a continued activist posture in the Middle East and elsewhere, given our low military force levels, the administration's unilateralist bent and unwillingness to budget more resources, especially in the face of others' suspicions and distrust of our actions?

The U.S. moved against the Taliban and Al Qaeda in Afghanistan in 2001 as everyone expected. This was widely accepted by the international community—after all, we had suffered a surprise attack, just as we had at Pearl Harbor. The U.S. had the moral backing of the international community, and chased the Taliban away from the power centers in Afghanistan, and helped the Afghans to set up a new government—all this with substantial NATO help. We almost destroyed Al Qaeda leadership at Tora Bora, but many escaped because they were better prepared that we thought they were and we failed to muster enough forces to completely surround them and crush them. So they slipped away, to regroup in Pakistan and later to send organizers to Iraq, and finally in 2006 returned to Afghanistan in force.[7]

Instead of focusing on the rebuilding of Afghanistan and the full destruction of Al Qaeda in 2002, the U.S. began preparations to remove Saddam Hussein from power in Iraq. Our traditional allies had substantial reservations about this, as did many Americans including Secretary of State Colin Powell.

Our intelligence services provided information that was warped to fit policymakers' views, and was just flat out wrong in many respects.[8] The president insisted Iraq had weapons of mass destruction—even though none were found after the invasion. Iraq was linked to the 9/11 terrorism even though Saddam had held Al Qaeda at arms length. Perhaps more important for American

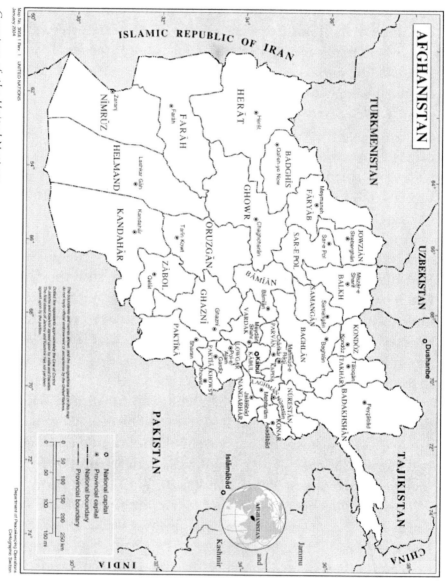

policy, the president and others spoke of extending democracy to the Middle East by military force.[9]

A number of military men and defense scholars have pointed out that the U.S. deployed way too few troops—hence the nightmare security situation on the ground in Iraq since May 2003. This happened despite warnings from the Army Chief of Staff that a force of between three hundred thousand and four hundred thousand would be needed to secure the peace. In retrospect, even the best contemporary history of the war suggests that the war itself was not enough to reestablish peace without a major, well-planned effort to rebuild Iraq.[10]

Even more depressing was the complete lack of preparation for the postwar effort. The U.S. government had not planned well, if at all, for the post-war phase. Full responsibility was assigned to, then seized by, the defense department. Those who managed the process did not understand the complex political/cultural reality of Iraq and pridefully refused to listen to those who did.[11]

Much of this lack of planning and understanding stems from a sense of arrogance on the part of key civilian leaders. Driven by the neoconservative ideology of bringing freedom to the Middle East by unilateral action, a freedom that they alleged would be welcomed by all, they pressed forward. America's natural pragmatism foundered on a lack of sound strategy and preparation. In simple common sense terms, we just weren't very good at what we were trying to do. We didn't seek information and refused to listen to those diplomats and military officers who cautioned us.

In the previous sixty years America led the world as a coalition leader, not as a unilateral know-it-all—which became the pattern after February 2002.

In the post-9/11 period, key civilians—the neoconservatives, Vice President Cheney, Secretary of Defense Rumsfeld, Deputy Secretary of Defense Wolfowitz, Undersecretary of Defense

Douglas Feith, perennial bulldog Richard Pearle—and others captured the ear of the president and urged war. None of these folks listened to the experts—or even to their own secretary of state.[12] Feith refused to use any of the State Department's arabists who had served on the group. There was little common sense, and less professionalism applied by rigid defense department officials.

What are the basic assumptions of this "neocon" policy, which have yet to be modified or repudiated? To state them is to define the problem:

- The U.S. has disproportionately great economic and military power and can act effectively without having to accommodate the view of others, including its allies.

- The 9/11 tragedy overturned historical rules of international behavior.

- As a global hegemon, the U.S. should not be constrained by international agreements which limit its course of action.

- Military action is more effective and more certain than diplomatic activity.

- Democracies do not launch wars, so the U.S. should press actively for democratization, especially in the Middle East, the center of Islamic terrorism (even if this involves making war!).

- As a Christian nation with a devout government, the U.S. enjoys a special moral authority.[13]

The damage this mindset has done has already jeopardized America's position, eroded its legitimacy internationally and reduced trust. If not soon modified or severely altered, it will take our country down an unfamiliar and historically dangerous path. This will cause permanent damage to America's international leadership, which has built and managed the sixty-year consensus around which the free world has rallied,[14] free of major armed conflict.

Primacy is not something new for Americans. Indeed, and perhaps unfortunately, the concept of American primacy almost seems to come too naturally. From the earliest days of the Republic we claimed that our institutions were fundamentally different from those of the rest of the civilized (and uncivilized) world. We were a "City Upon a Hill," the "New Jerusalem," and a beacon for humankind. We asserted a primacy for our values of life, liberty and the pursuit of happiness. As our national power grew in the late nineteenth and early twentieth centuries we were less and less content to be merely a beacon for democracy. Increasingly we sought to make ourselves into a missionary force for those values. To be sure, there were voices of caution. Early on, President George Washington urged us to beware of permanent alliances with the powers of Europe, as it would endanger our own freedom.

President John Quincy Adams told Americans:

> The United States does not go abroad in search of monsters to destroy. She will recommend the general cause of freedom and independence by the consistency of her voice and by the benign sympathy of her example.

But by the end of the nineteenth century, the conviction of its Manifest Destiny was well-entrenched in America's self-image, reinforced by America's spectacularly swift victory over Spain in 1898.

President Theodore Roosevelt's dispatch of the Great White Fleet on a voyage around the world in 1907— following his peacemaking between Russia and Japan in 1905—announced America's arrival. Imagine if you will, a fleet of sixteen

**President
John Quincy Adams**
*Source: Library of
Congress*

white battleships on a forty thousand-mile cruise, touching every continent, circumnavigating the globe. It was a massive demonstration of American power. The purpose of this grand gesture was to make the world understand that America had joined the ranks of the great naval powers and could, in that area at least, rival both the British and the Germans.

Great White Fleet—USS Kansas sails ahead of the USS Vermont as the fleet leaves Hampton Roads, Virginia on December 16, 1907.
Source: Wikipedia

However, neoconservatives ignored Roosevelt's diplomatic skills and activities—he won the Nobel Prize for making peace between Russia and Japan, and was deeply concerned about world order.[15]

The Wilsonian interlude before the First World War continued in the same vein—producing an active interventionist policy to support democratic governments ("We will teach them to elect good men"), and the idealism of democracy. But Wilson wanted to carry out his policies through international organizations and collective security, while the neoconservatives of today seek to use American power to enforce their views unilaterally. Their impact is completely different and more negative toward others than their Wilsonian model.

World War I brought America's first participation in a European conflict. Our intervention brought the war to a successful (for our allies) conclusion. We had participated as an "associated power" with Britain, France and Italy, in a "war to end all wars." Woodrow Wilson then tried to commit us to an enduring peace settlement that he hoped would make the world safe for democracy through an active internationalist policy focusing on collective security.[16] But the U.S. had tired of its first foray into great power, world politics and war, and focused inward upon itself in the 1920s and 30s. However, the country could not escape the fact that it was one of the two most potentially powerful nations on the globe.

The U.S. by this point had already created the world's most powerful economy. As a result of World War I, we became the world's leading creditor, the engine of world growth. American economic primacy was on the horizon. But we did not yet have the maturity or position to claim political or military primacy, and our people were certainly not ready to support a major international role in the inter-war period of isolationism. The totalitarian powers of Europe joined with militaristic Japan, and the Second World War came. Again the Americans came to the rescue.

World War II consolidated America's global position of leadership. Europe was devastated. Its colonial empires were in their last years. The U.S. was the unchallenged political and economic leader of the free world, with fifty percent of total global production in 1945. Our economy continued to grow at a prodigious rate. Europe did, of course, recover from the devastation of the war, but only with the help of the Marshall Plan and enhanced U.S. participation in international security affairs. We supported the UN, but went beyond that with bilateral pacts with key countries and the creation of NATO ("to keep the Russians out and the Germans in," remarked Europeans under their breath). Liberal internationalism replaced prewar isolation. Unapologetically the United States assumed the burden of containing communism.[17] We created a network of alliances, NATO, CENTO, SEATO and ANZUS that consolidated our primacy in the non-communist world.

Even in the U.S.-Soviet bipolar world of the '50s and '60s the U.S. was first among equals. The Soviet Union could seek to match us militarily and in space, but the Soviet economy was never even close to ours. We learned later that its military was also significantly less powerful than once thought.

The collapse of communism, symbolized by the fall of the Berlin Wall, left America in the unique situation of being the sole superpower, a position in which we still find ourselves. The challenge, which we have faced in the last decade, since the collapse of communism and particularly in the aftermath of 9/11, is how to exercise that power, and in the service of what values. Adjusting to the new times has been difficult. Americans were proud of our own leadership, but an "American Empire?" America destroyed empires; it didn't create them. We conveniently forgot about the lessons from our role in the Philippines in 1899—a bloody fourteen-year war to suppress the people we helped liberate

EUROPEAN UNION

Courtesy of The Universtiy of Texas Libraries, The University of Texas at Austin

from Spain—as well as the failures of President Woodrow Wilson's attempts to teach self-government to our Latin neighbors in his first administration. Less than thirty years away from the end of the Vietnamese War in 1975, we again had collective amnesia about the insurgent war of that period and failed to prepare properly for Iraq.

The neoconservatives married Wilsonian idealism to *realpolitik* and revived the talk of "empire"—America was the strongest power in the world and needed to flex its muscles. The word didn't fit exactly, but Charles Krauthamer spoke eloquently of the "unipolar moment" and the phrase stuck.[18] But neither politicians nor ideologues raised the question of what that might cost and what it would mean to our values.

President Theodore Roosevelt
Source: Wikipedia, photo by Pach Brothers

Americans paid too little attention to history and our own backlash against imperial activity. Even Theodore Roosevelt, a very under-appreciated and misrepresented president by the way, turned against the early twentieth century imperial experiment quickly. In 1910, asked whether the U.S. should annex the Dominican Republic, he commented:

> As for annexing the island [Dominican Republic], I have about the same desire to annex it as a gorged boa constrictor might have to swallow a porcupine wrong-end-to.[19]

President Franklin Delano Roosevelt
Source: Wikipedia, photo by Elias Goldensky

Franklin Roosevelt's Good Neighbor policy in the 1930s reversed some of the legacy of the early years of the century with respect to Latin America, but the

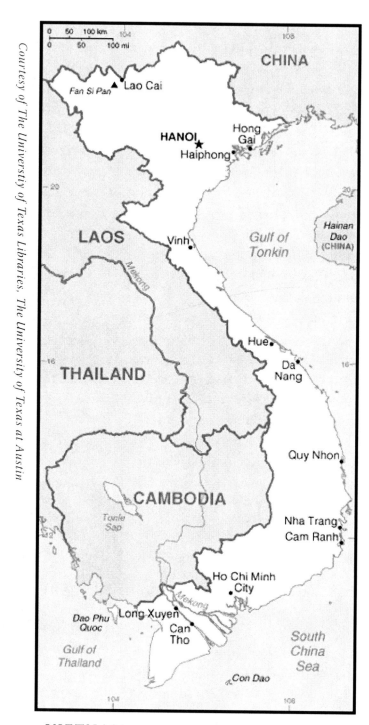

VIETNAM

world was quickly caught up in the evils of Japanese and German expansionism.

Failure to complete the dismantling of imperialism after World War II led France and later the U.S. (God must think we're slow learners) into a major quagmire in Vietnam—which much of the American leadership seems to have forgotten, as the insurgency continues to function in Iraq in the summer of 2008.[20] The growing awakening of formerly docile populations has made conquest terribly expensive and at least impracticable, if not impossible.

While we didn't create it, the European imperial legacy is an important element of our current problems in the Middle East. There, the U.S. is seen, rightly or wrongly, as Britain's successor by most of those who would otherwise appreciate, if not admire, our values. While we viewed our invasion of Iraq as bringing freedom, the overwhelming majority of those in the region saw it as the same old story of imperial conquest. In fact, approval of America dropped to single digits in every country except Israel and Iran where the younger 65 percent of the population dislikes the ayatollahs and rather fancies the U.S., though this rating has dropped to around 50 percent or below in the past year as the U.S. has put more pressure on Iran over its nuclear production.

President George H.W. Bush, operating in the post-Cold War environment, pulled allies, including Arab states, together to help pay for Gulf War I, in stark contrast to his son's efforts in 2003. President Bill Clinton ironically wound up intervening in more places than the first Bush (Haiti, Bosnia, Yugoslavia, and attacks on Afghanistan and Somalia). Neoconservatives seized upon the post-9/11 situation to challenge the whole idea of international law, multilateral internationalism and the idea of the U.S.

President George Herbert Walker Bush
Source: Wikipedia

Paul Wolfowitz, former Deputy Secretary of Defense
Source: National Communications System

as leader of a coalition. Neoconservative spokesmen Max Boot, William Kristol and Paul Wolfowitz all argued the U.S. should embrace the idea of primacy if not "empire."[21] Few Americans really understand what a major change this has brought to American policy and the potential resistance it engenders. The overwhelming majority of Americans that I have spoken with over the past few years are repelled by the ideal of imperial conquest and what it implies for the nation.

But the devil is, as usual, in the details. The threat of Al Qaeda and its associated networks was stimulated by a reaction to U.S. "imperialism," and Arabs and Iraqis of many stripes reacted much more negatively to the U.S. military conquest that the neoconservatives had imagined.

Middle East specialists and others realized immediately the unfortunate implications of U.S. actions—but the administration consulted no one who did not already share its unilateralist views.[22]

In their arrogance, Defense officials Feith and Wolfowitz ignored and excluded the 112-person State Department planning team for post-Saddam Iraq from all Defense Department planning for the transition to peace. This team had begun at The Brookings Institution, then moved into the State Department and produced a thirteen-volume work that is still classified. Those who have read it say that the team's effort anticipated virtually all of the problems the Coalition Provisional Authority (CPA) faced. The plan was never considered, and the key people—our key cadre of Arabic speakers who wrote it—were initially *forbidden* to go out to Iraq with General Garner's original team in April 2003. Some resurfaced when Paul Bremer became the CPA chief in mid-2003, but valuable and critical time had been lost.

Under Bremer, the U.S. persisted in major mistakes:

1. The strategy of attacking Iraq to stop terror and help the Arab/Israeli peace process worsened the terror and failed to stop weapons flowing to the Palestinian radicals;

2. We used a false rationale to justify the attack—there were no significant WMDs, a problem that has bedeviled

IRAQ

Courtesy of The Universtiy of Texas Libraries, The University of Texas at Austin

American intelligence since the first Bush administration and the Clinton terms;

3. We failed to significantly internationalize the effort, leaving us saddled with overwhelming costs, whereas the first President Bush arranged for allies to pay much of the cost for Gulf War I;

4. Department of Defense planners woefully underestimated the task and just assumed that all would flock to our standard;

5. We trusted the exiles and bought into their bogus "intelligence," while the exiles gave our secrets to the Iranians;

6. We lacked serious planning—we demobilized the Iraqi army, and we had no adequate nation-building or civil affairs structure to put in place; and

7. We had too few troops to complete the job.

The size of the original provisional authority sent to Iraq, former U. S. Central Command (CENTCOM) chief General Tony Zinni

Gen. Anthony Charles Zinni, former Commander in Chief of U.S. Central Command (CENTCOM)
Source: Wikipedia

estimates, was about 1/20th of what earlier planning had established as necessary to reshape the country successfully.[23]

Neoconservative assertions that U.S. troops would be welcomed in Iraq with open arms and embrace the conquerors were a sad echo of 1899, when Manila's upper classes told President McKinley "not to worry about the nationalists," and when Catholic South Vietnamese leaders told our forces there that the Buddhists were "politically insignificant."

The result thus far in Iraq has been engagement with a Middle Eastern tar baby with either no (or a bad) end in sight, plus a precipitous decline in American prestige and respect across the board. It is clear that America's ability to transform societies now remains very limited, in large part by our own ineptitude.[24] Echoing John Quincy Adams, some even say that in seeking to unilaterally search and destroy monsters, we have become one ourselves.

President William McKinley
Source: Wikipedia

Note carefully, however—it is the unilateralism that irritates allies and infuriates others more than just the U.S. being powerful. For sixty years, a sizable portion of the world accepted and relied on U.S. power—when exercised with tact, diplomacy and concern for others in the international system. Within the past few years, we have seen our public approval ratings bottom out, and growing discord in our major alliances. Americans cannot exercise primacy by bullying others, and remain true to their own values. Others, though, cannot do without U.S. power without risking international anarchy, or else it will be the 1930s all over again, with new challengers and near anarchy.

Today, post-9/11 and post-Iraq, American primacy is attacked by new, non-state challengers—Al Qaeda and other terrorist networks. These are not classic challenges from countries, and they require both new, subtler strategies and a renewed concern for and understanding of other peoples.

POWER AND DIPLOMACY

Power, of course, is not the same as primacy, nor is primacy merely a question of power. Indeed, we need to be very clear about the different kinds of means at our disposal, for what ends we propose to use them, and what strategies we adopt.

Military power

There can be no question that we enjoy a unique military superiority. In recent years this superiority has been demonstrated in Bosnia, Kosovo, Afghanistan and Iraq. Neither our enemies nor our allies have comparable military capabilities. The U.S. spends about 45 percent of the world's investments in military outlay. No other country can match the commitment we have made, and continue to make, in weapons systems. For purposes of conventional war we are not equaled and we cannot be defeated— though we may lose the will to fight. Unfortunately, the shock of 9/11, has led to American hubris overpowering traditional American self-confident prudence.

Whether our military capabilities are appropriate for the undeclared and unconventional war against global terrorism is another question. Aircraft carriers, battle tanks, smart bombs and a dominant nuclear capability are only part of what we need to protect ourselves against the kinds of attacks we faced on 9/11.[25]

We evidently have the capacity to intervene intensively in *one* conflict anywhere in the world, but it is a serious question whether we can do *two* such interventions. From a common sense point of view, with forces committed across the globe, and the government using the National Guard as part of the Regular Army presence in Iraq, we have *no* extra capacity to carry out major sustained actions against Iran or North Korea, with whom we are dickering over nuclear issues. It would require enacting a draft law and waiting through a prolonged buildup.

It is even less clear how, or even if, we can use our military power effectively in the struggle against transnational or non-state-sponsored terrorism.

Counter-terrorism is a complex political struggle that requires political and diplomatic skill, economic power, the "soft" power of culture, and the ability to rally the world community around values we all agree upon.[26] Virtually all serious commentators who are not ideological neoconservatives believe a great deal more diplomacy needs to be brought into play than we are using today. Even trenchant State Department political critic and bully Newt Gingrich called for more money for diplomacy, more regional expertise, and a 40 percent increase in personnel.[27]

Do we have the weapons systems, tactics and strategies we need to counter the terrorist threat—which requires more combined police work than sustained force? Even if we have these, do we have the political will to build coalitions to exercise that power in a focused and meaningful way for a sufficient length of time to prevail? Since the beginning of 2004, there has been an increasing clamor from the professional foreign affairs community that there must be a better way to proceed. Despite the president's continued insistence on the correctness of his Iraqi policy, the din and the casualties continue. We are about to turn error into folly (see next chapter) and achieve disaster.

We inevitably will have to take the lead in exercising our power against a variety of new threats, both the spread of international terrorism and the dangers associated with the proliferation of weapons of mass destruction. How we do it is crucial, however. We cannot obtain the critical international cooperation and support that we need if we try to go it alone in an imperious manner. Persuasion, diplomacy and broader support are essential. All other empires either learned, or were forced to learn this lesson.[28]

There are some useful precedents. Europe faced a similar but secular kind of multinational terrorist threat in the early 1970s in the Red Brigades and the Bader-Meinhof gangs. By careful police, intelligence and paramilitary work, plus excellent international cooperation, that threat was first contained, and then destroyed. That is the way the current threat should and will finally have to be contained and removed.

ECONOMIC POWER

Economic issues are the most problematic for those who boast of American Primacy. We are the third most populous nation, and our economy is—at least for now—the largest on the globe. We have the highest productivity, and the largest single share of Gross National Product (GNP), yet we are less confident about the overall welfare of the economy, for good reasons: The U.S. has a growing dependency on foreign oil and foreign capital that relies on respect for its financial institutions and policies. Domestically, issues of globalization and production are center-stage, yet American wages are stagnant.[29]

China is a major factor in both capital dependency and globalization. China holds massive amounts of the U.S. debt and carries a huge trade surplus with us. Leaving aside political issues such as the status of Taiwan and North Korean nuclear weapons, the 2005.

A re-evaluation of the Chinese Yuan sent shock waves through the Western financial community. The Yuan is no longer linked to the dollar, and financial experts expect it to rise in value over time. If it is allowed (by the Chinese) to rise *too* sharply, it will push bond yields higher and seriously hurt the U.S. economy.

If the Chinese reduce purchases of U.S. bonds it could also cause growing economic problems here as well, including inflation and higher interest rates. In sum, we have less control over our own economic future than we used to.

Moreover, in terms of energy, China and India are using more oil every year, straining existing capacity and driving prices up—beyond $100 a barrel in the spring of 2008 to $140 by summer. The reality is that growing oil needs worldwide, but especially in China and India, are going to steeply increase the price of fuel and transportation, driving gas prices even further up. This time there is an ugly political twist: most of those revenues will go to two states—Iran and Saudi Arabia, the world's first and second oil exporters, who are currently awash in cash, which in the past has often found its way to terrorist groups.

The above is a glum but very realistic scenario—unless, at the current price we can develop bio-fuels, better bicycles and superior public transportation. There is going to be a worldwide shortage of fossil fuel, and nothing much has yet been done about it beyond experimental programs.

It doesn't take much common sense and good judgment to see that a unilateralist foreign policy stressing American primacy is probably not going to give us the best leverage to deal with these kinds of issues, where cooperation is essential to getting workable solutions.

There can be little doubt that controversy continues about globalization, trade, jobs and outsourcing. All these topics reflect a profound sense of uncertainty and malaise among our fellow citizens. We do not feel ourselves to be all-powerful in the face of globalization. It does not help to be told that we are number one, when the benefits of being number one seem so fragile, so fleeting, and so unevenly distributed, and our mortgage market is failing. Moreover, key private financial leaders are suggesting that we are seriously overstretched, with potentially disastrous consequences if we do not get better control of our economic affairs and stop spending beyond reasonable limits.[30] Recent dollar fluctuations have renewed this argument, and even fiscally conservative Republicans are deserting the president.

America's economic primacy may not endure, and it would be nice, if not essential, to have some friends when it is gone; even better to pay some attention now to reversing or slowing the decline. While China and India are not competitors for primacy now, a half a century from now will certainly offer a different picture.

Soft Power

Joseph Nye, dean of the John F. Kennedy School at Harvard, stresses the necessity of emphasizing America's "soft power." He correctly asserts that our soft power is as important as the hard military and economic strength, all of which go to make up the principal pillars of America's primacy.[31]

The elements of soft power are easy to find—three American music companies produce 85 percent of the music sold around the world, our cultural influence is, for better or worse, ubiquitous— MTV, Spielberg, McDonald's, Madonna, Angelina Jolie. For better or worse, we're *there*. Although this can be one of the reasons people react against us, it can also be a powerful source of strength. In both China and India, over 90 percent say English is the most important second language to learn.

The challenge we face is how to use the strength of our values and our commitment to freedom and justice in ways that enhance America's national interests, not subtract from them—as is the case now in several areas. This will require skillful public diplomacy as we seek to project our values in a positive way, and it will take time. Changing the attitudes of a whole generation of young militant Muslims in the Arab World, in Pakistan, Afghanistan and beyond is not the work of a single year—or even a single presidential term. Our own educational system has not yet caught up with our role in the world, and we need to learn more history, culture and languages if we are gong to be effective in the world.

Moral influence

This is the other source of power, but this can be a two-edged sword. The State Department's current five-year strategic plan contains these words:

> U.S. values and interests drive our policies. Moreover the values we espouse of political

and economic freedom and the non-negotiable demands of humanity are increasingly recognized as universal rather than culturally specified.

President Bush at the end of his 2004 State of the Union address stated:

The cause we serve is right because it is the cause of all mankind. The momentum of freedom in our world is unmistakable and it is not carried forward by our power alone. We can trust in that greater power who guides the unfolding of the years. And in all that is to come, we can know that His purposes are just and true.

These two quotes echo the long tradition of American exceptionalism, the call to exert moral leadership in the world. In it are combined the twin themes that have animated presidents from the earliest days of the republic, and particularly in the twentieth century: that American values act as a beacon of hope for the world and that America has a missionary obligation to make those values available to others.

But there is another aspect of this story, dangers represented by the Abu Ghraib prison scandals—our failure to live up to

Abu Ghraib Cell Block prior to reconstruction
Source: www.usdoj.gov/oig/special/0502/ February 2005, Office of the Inspector General

our own best ideals. Americans of all faiths have returned from journeys to all parts of the world in the past few years stunned by the universally negative perceptions of America and its values, especially among the world's Muslims, but even among America's traditional friends. Clearly, we must look critically at how we live our values and their impact on others. Often the freedom we enjoy is seen as libertinism, the economic success that we have achieved is viewed as exploitation of others, and our military might appears as a tool for cultural and political domination.

There is also a deeper set of moral issues, first raised a half-century ago by Reinhold Niebuhr, America's premier twentieth century theologian, in *The Irony of American History*. He focused on the moral ambiguity of building nuclear weapons to preserve peace, and the need to examine our own actions very clearly and objectively, understanding the clear moral issues raised by extending our power in the search of valuable goals we seek.[32]

Andrew Bacevich, a former military officer now a student of empire, brings Niebuhr's irony forward to the present: in our present efforts to build an earthly democratic paradise we are in danger of donning moral blinders so that it becomes "not simply a fantasy, but a positive danger, giving rise to arrogance and self-righteousness."[33]

In seeking to impose a *Pax Americana* on the world, we should seek to understand what that may really mean—killing children who carry bombs, more Abu Ghraibs. As we examine our purpose, said Niebuhr, we need to have "a sense of modesty about the virtue, wisdom and power available to us for the resolution of it perplexities."[34] If we cannot do this, we will indeed have become the monsters John Quincy Adams spoke of.

Christian churches are wrestling with the implications of Just War and Just Peace. We have not really had to come to terms with the moral component of our power since the early days of the Cold War. In Vietnam, we faced the moral ambiguity of fighting a nationalist insurgency and it almost shredded our national consensus.

Now, deeply into Iraq, the irony has returned, and our moral dilemmas cannot all be answered with force capability and unilateral will.

Most of us do not want to continue the search for unilateral primacy, especially if the cost is dishonoring our heritage, expending vast sums needed for domestic issues, and expanding our military. Many are troubled that we are not "playing well with others." These are entirely common sense reactions to America's stake in the world and our leaders' minimizing diplomacy in recent years. We will return to this theme later, after exploring some additional elements of difficulty in the contemporary world of diplomacy. But it is important to understand that the issue, "primacy: condition or policy?" underlies everything we do in our international life.

---

[1] Bacevich, A.J. *American Empire*. (Cambridge: Harvard University Press, 2002), chs. 1-2; Ferguson, Niall. *Colossus: The Price of America's Empire*. New York: The Penguin Press (2004), chs. 1, 4 and conclusion, pp. 286-302; Merry, Robert W. *Sands of Empire*, (New York: Simon & Schuster (2005), chs. 2, 11, 13 and conclusion, pp. 251-254. On neoconservatives views, see Kaplan, Fred. *Daydream Believers*. New York: John Wiley & Sons (2008), especially chs. 1, 5 and 6.

[2] Woodward, Bob. *State of Denial*. (New York: Simon and Schuster, 2006), pp. 370-1.

[3] "How the 'Good War' in Afghanistan Went Bad," The New York Times, August 12, 2007, p. 1.

[4] The best description of the European view can be found in Todd, E. *After the Empire*. (New York, Columbia University Press, 2002), chs. 1, 3 and conclusion, pp. 191-202; and Kaplan, Robert D. *An Empire in the Wilderness* (New York: Vintage Books, 1998), chs. 1 and 6.

[5] Hentz, J.J. *The Obligation of Empire: United States' Grand Strategy for a New Century* (Lexington, Univ. of Kentucky Press, 2004 ch. 4. "What is within our powers?" Walter Russell Mead (2004), *Power, Terror, Peace and War*. (Knopf, New York, 2004), chs. 1, 4, 11 and 12.

[6] Ferguson, op. cit., (2004), pp. 3-29 and Merry, op. cit., (2005), pp. 220-31.

[7] Coll, Steve. *Ghost Wars: The Secret History of the CIA, Afghanistan and bin Laden, from the Soviet Invasion to September 10, 2001* (New York: Penguin Books, 2004).

[8] Bamford, J. *A Pretext for War* (New York: Doubleday/Random House, 2004), pp. 372-77; and Tenet, George. *At the Center of the Storm* (New York: HarperCollins, 2007), chs. 21 and 22.

[9] Bamford, op. cit., chs. 1-3; and Anonymous (2004). *Imperial Hubris: Why the West is losing the war on terror.* (Washington: Brassey's Inc.), ch. 2 and conclusion, pp. 261-64; Kean, Thomas H. and Lee Hamilton. "Intelligence Reform can not wait," *Louisville Courier-Journal,* September 12, 2004 p. H-1.

[10] Murray, W. and R. J. Scales, Jr. *The Iraq War.* (2003) Cambridge: The Belknap Press of Harvard University Press, especially ch. 7, "Military and Political Implications." Zinni, Anthony, Center for Defense Information. "Eye on Iraq," May 22, 2004 and "Gen. Zinni: 'They've Screwed Up,'" http://www.cbsnews.com/stories/2004/04/21/60minutes/printable618896.shtml

[11] Diamond, Larry. *Squandered Victory.* (New York: Henry Holt & Co., 2005) pp. 1-10 and ch. 10.

[12] Woodward, B. *Plan of Attack.* (New York: Simon and Schuster, 2004) ch. 34, and Lindsay, J.M. and Daalder, I.H. *American Unbound: The Bush Revolution in Foreign Policy* (Washington: The Brookings Institution Press, 2003), pp. 130-5.

[13] Points partially based on those in an article by Harrop, William C. "Major International Challenges the U.S. will Face in 2005," in the Internet journal, www.americandiplomacy.org.

[14] Tucker, R.W. and D.C. Hendrickson. *"The Sources of American Legitimacy" Foreign Affairs.* November/December 2004, vol. 83, no. 6, pp. 18-32. Odom, William and Richard Dujarric. *America's Inadvertent Empire.* (New Haven: Yale Univ. Press, 2004), ch. 3 and pp. 204-18.

[15] Holmes, James R. *Theodore Roosevelt and World Order.* (Washington: Potomac Books, 2006), especially chs. 8-10.

[16] Magstadt, T.M. *An Empire If You Can Keep It.* (Washington: CQ Press, 2004), chs. 1-3.

[17] Spalding, E.E. *The First Cold Warrior: Harry Truman, Containment, and the Remaking of Liberal Internationalism* (Lexington: University Press of Kentucky, 2006), chs. 4-6.

[18] Krauthamer, Charles, "The Unipolar Moment Revisited." *The National Interest,* Winter 2002/3, pp. 5-17.

[19] I am indebted to Ambassador Tony Quainton for this quote as well as other thoughts on this subject.

[20] Burns, J.F. and E. Eckholm. "In Western Iraq, Fundamentalists Hold U.S. at Bay," *The New York Times,* Aug. 29, 2004. p. 1.

[21] Boot, M. *The Savage Wars of Peace.* (New York: Basic Books, 2002).

[22] This is a strong statement, but I have two different sources who polled a list of three hundred-plus Middle East experts—none had been consulted.

[23] Compiled from a survey of discussions on this point. The Zinni point comes from his extremely thoughtful remarks to the Center for Defense Information Board, which can be found at www.cdi.org

[24] Diamond, L. "What Went Wrong in Iraq." *Foreign Affairs*, September/October 2004, pp. 34-56.

[25] Anonymous (2004), op. cit. chs. 6-8; and Odom (2004), op. cit. ch. 3, "The Military Power Gap."

[26] Joes, A. *America and Guerilla Warfare.* (Lexington: University Press of Kentucky, 2000), pp. 1-4 and 318-32; and also his *Resisting Rebellion.* (2004), University Press of Kentucky, pp. 218-59.

[27] Gingrich, N. "Rogue State Department." *Foreign Policy*, July-August 2003, pp. 42-48.

[28] Ferguson (2004), op. cit. pp. 286-302; Merry (2005), op. cit. pp. 3-39.

[29] Mead, W.R. "America's Sticky Power." *Foreign Policy*, March/April 2004 pp. 46-53.

[30] Summers, L.H. "America Overdrawn." *Foreign Policy*, July/August 2004, pp. 46-49; and Peterson, P. "Riding for a Fall." *Foreign Affairs*, September/October 2004, pp. 111-15,

[31] Nye, J.S. Jr. *The Paradox of American Power.* (New York: Oxford University Press, 2002), chs. 1 and 5; and Nye, Soft Power (New York: Public Affairs Press, 2004, chs. 1-3.

[32] Niebuhr, R. *The Irony of American History.* (1962 edition) New York: Charles Scribner's Sons. especially chs. 1 and 7.

[33] Bacevich, A. "Conclusion: Reinhold Niebuhr and the Hazards of Empire," in Hentz, op. cit. p. 200.

[34] Niebuhr, R. op. cit., p. 174.

CHAPTER 3
ERROR, FOLLY & INTELLIGENCE

---

*It ain't what you don't know that will hurt you; it's what you think
you know that ain't so.*

—Abe Martin (Kin Hubbard)

ABE MARTIN, KIN HUBBARD'S FICTIONAL INDIANA SAGE,
captured the essence of the problem policy makers have with
intelligence. Intelligence gathering is entwined with that of nations
and governments throughout history. People and governments
don't like surprises, and both individuals and organizations believe
the more information they have, the better off they will be. A
corollary is that, given the laws of human nature, people will try to
hide facts or feed others incorrect information when they believe
it is to their advantage, and they think they can get away with
it. Hence intelligence organizations are created to obtain such
information, and counterintelligence units arise to protect it.

Some problems in this paradigm have consistently arisen
across history. First, the possibility of erroneous or misleading
information creates a problem of credibility. Second, the analysis
used to prepare information has been flawed, producing poor
advice and differences that hamstring governments which
occasionally (some say often) lead to error, and then to folly.

Third is a policy/decision making issue much broader
than the other two. At key junctures of history, error has been

compounded by stubbornness over time by individuals and organizations to produce what historian Barbara Tuchman calls "folly." She made this distinction in discussing historical errors that were compounded into folly and disaster:[1] *Folly is the continued persistence of error to produce action, usually adverse, which fails to accomplish the desired goals and eventually leads to disaster for those persisting in it.*

Common sense tells us that the descent from error into folly should be strenuously avoided. The reality is not that easy. In the context of the American political system, such a march to folly is more common and costly than we would wish. As the U.S. has attained "sole superpower" status, bluster, hubris and arrogance make it more difficult to admit error in the first place, especially if one's party has an overwhelming dominance of both the congressional and the executive branch. Part of America's problem here is that we have come late to the use of intelligence and have moral scruples about the unsavory side of intelligence work. Historically, the American political system disregarded the need for systemic, formal, organized intelligence gathering by not developing any for nearly one hundred years.

President George Washington
Source: University of Texas Libraries, The University of Texas at Austin

George Washington created his own informal intelligence network during the American Revolution, but it dissolved after the American victory at Yorktown. The U.S. Army began to develop intelligence units during and after the Civil War, including experimenting with outsourcing intelligence to The Pinkerton Agency. Formal organizations were not created until the 1880s by the Army and Navy departments.

In World War I, the military services ran their own programs, and a civilian

Committee on Public Information under George Creel focused largely on propaganda and internal security. During the interwar years 1919-1939, American intelligence lapsed back into previous peacetime routines, with the military service units dominating the field. U.S. State Department code-breaking efforts were terminated in 1929 because Secretary of State Henry Stimson felt it was "ungentlemanly" to read others' mail.

**President
Harry S. Truman**
*Source: Wikipedia,
Photo by U. S. Army
Signal Corps*

As the war clouds grew over Europe again in the late 1930s, President Franklin Roosevelt selected William O. Donovan to create the Office of the Coordinator of Information (OCI) in June 1941, which became the Office of Strategic Services (OSS) the next year. This was the first organized American effort to conduct what became known within the next decade as "covert activities"—propaganda, political operations, economic operations and paramilitary activities—as well as sabotage, espionage and counterespionage during World War II.

Until this point Americans generally had grown to believe intelligence was somehow immoral (though this never bothered our founding fathers), and the relative safety of the American nation separated from hostile powers by two oceans was sufficient to prevent the country from abandoning this notion until December 7, 1941, when the Japanese surprise attack on Pearl Harbor destroyed much of our fleet and our illusion of invincibility.

When OSS was disbanded in September 1945, President Truman transferred its intelligence functions to the State Department, where they became State's Bureau of Intelligence and Research. He also created the Central Intelligence Group (CIG) a year later to keep the rest of the trained professionals, including covert action operators, together until the U.S. could sort out its postwar needs.[2]

Most of today's scholarly work cites the creation of the CIA in 1947 by the National Security Act as the real beginning of permanent, professionalized intelligence in the American government.[3] The vast increase in technological capabilities—better communications, satellite photography, etc., required a much greater concentration of resources and manpower to succeed. Cooperation with Allied intelligence services in World War II had socialized American military officers and diplomats to international intelligence work. The imperatives of post-war politics and the rise of the Cold War made such an effort necessary on a broader and continuing basis.[4]

Post-World War II, intelligence activities became linked with covert operations—undercover efforts to shape the political environment that, as a distinguished former CIA director said, "required only five percent of our budget, but created 95 percent of our difficulties with Congress and the President."[5]

The CIA maintained links with the State Department and the military in Washington. Abroad, U.S. and other countries' embassies often hosted resident personnel under "official" cover. The Agency and the military pioneered round-the-clock alert centers. The U.S. State Department did not develop a 24-hour crisis management/ intelligence center until 1961, in the aftermath of the Cuban Missile Crisis. The overall tension between the utility of covert action and the requirements of diplomacy and foreign policy continue to this day, breaking out in open hostility on occasion and potentially contributing to errors.

Because covert action is such a special case of intelligence activity, a precise definition is helpful:

Covert action, also known as "special activities," includes any operation designed to influence foreign governments, persons, or events in support of the sponsoring government's foreign policy objectives while keeping the sponsoring government's support of the operation secret. Whereas in clandestine collection, the emphasis is on keeping the activity secret, in covert action the emphasis is on keeping the sponsorship secret.[6]

Such activities are aimed at keeping the sponsoring government's role secret, but they also violate the diplomatic Vienna Convention injunctions against interference in the domestic affairs of the host country. When a covert action is uncovered, the sponsoring country's relations with the target country are adversely affected. This generally brings diplomats back into the problem since they are the ones who take the brunt of criticism and later raise the general foreign policy question of whether such actions are worth the cost. Hence, some consider covert action immoral; however, all U.S. presidents since Franklin Roosevelt have used it, and several before him.

As covert action became a bureaucratized activity in U.S. foreign policy after World War II, it became controversial. For over twenty-five years after 1945, during the Cold war, Americans treated covert activities with a "don't ask, don't tell" mentality. This followed a familiar, continuing pattern: most nations do not now and never have openly discussed their covert activities.

**Frank Church,
former U.S. Senator**
*Source: Wikipedia,
Biographical
Directory of the U.S.
Congress*

This began to change in the U.S. in the early 1970s when U.S. involvement in Chile drew the attention of Senator Frank Church and others, and in 1975-76 led to a congressional commission investigating alleged intelligence "abuses."[7] The Church commission and subsequent efforts have focused on three issues: Is covert action effective? Is covert action under control? Is covert action moral?

Analysis from both academic and professional sources stresses several negative points:

1. The "blowback," or adverse reaction by others to failed operations (or even successful ones) sometimes seriously damages U.S. foreign policy;

2. Americans are deficient in the cultural understanding necessary to successfully manipulate other cultures, hence covert action often ends badly;

3. Covert action is not an effective mechanism for resolving crises and has to be integrated as part of an effective policy to succeed;

4. Often the objectives of the covert activity are not compatible with American values;

5. Often unclear boundaries between covert action and military operations result in failures; and

6. Short-term successes often lead to long term disasters.[8]

Others, including some critics, concede that despite difficulties, covert action is something that can be useful if used properly:

1. If covert activities are integrated into coherent overall foreign policy;

2. If active coordination is maintained between all government agencies; and

3. If no overt options will accomplish the mission. Most agree that other options should be exhausted—much of the political and propaganda work should be done openly, and it must be done competently to produce a good chance of success. Like other choices for effective action, there are pitfalls as well as possibilities.[9]

The point is that covert action needs to be judged by the same strict criteria of judgment by which other policy options are assessed. Carried out in secret, denied by its originators, covert operations can sometimes succeed spectacularly—like U.S. operations against South Asian Communists in Laos in the early 1960s—or fail miserably, as they did at the Bay of Pigs in 1961, leaving us with the legacy of Fidel Castro for forty-five years and counting. Just because they are clandestine does not mean covert actions are not subject to the same rules of error and folly that apply to any other policy choice.

INDIVIDUAL ERRORS

Examples of individual errors are the mistakes that led or contributed significantly to Pearl Harbor, the Battle of the Bulge, the Iranian Revolution and the Gulf War. Beyond that are a category of follies in which errors of intelligence and judgment were compounded to produce the American Revolution, American involvement in Vietnam, and contemporary Iran-American relations.

Battle of the Bulge Bastogne, Belgium—Troops of the 101st Airborne Division watch C-47s drop supplies.

Source: www.history.army.mil

Follies and errors have their genesis in both individual and organizational failures or inadequacies. Individual deficiencies lay the groundwork for organizational problems. Rational theories of policy/decision making emphasize complete and extensive fact gathering and perception. Common sense tells us this is unlikely to be a perfect process. Individuals perceive events according to their own makeup and biases. Moreover, as the great English theologian C. S. Lewis put it so well:

> Five senses; an incurably abstract intellect; a haphazardly selective memory; a set of preconceptions and assumptions so numerous that I can never ex-

amine more than a minority of them—never become even conscious of them all. How much of total reality can such an apparatus let through?[10]

Often, both intelligence officers and policy makers misunderstand the cultures they are dealing with; the "facts" are very slippery and subjective; and the problems seldom have pure straight-line solutions. This should make people cautious and unwilling to jump to conclusions. Sadly this is not always the case with senior officials in any organization—business, government, or nor-profit organizations.

One of the best-known examples is December 1941. U.S. Army and Navy commanders in Hawaii were convinced that Japan would not attack Pearl Harbor. In the face of mounting evidence that something was afoot, they interpreted each new piece of intelligence according to their own preconceptions: The Japanese carriers could not be located because of radio silence—they were assumed to be headed for Malaya. Small, two-man submarines surfaced off Oahu very early Sunday, December 7—were considered simply reconnaissance. Radar reports of incoming aircraft—assumed to be American bombers arriving from the mainland.

An entire group of experienced U.S. military officers were so certain that Japan would not attack Pearl Harbor that they even decided not to alter the fleet and naval base training exercises to provide increased readiness and reconnaissance, disregarding entirely the possibility that they could be wrong, as well as the potential consequences if they were.

Similarly, Allied commanders in Europe in December 1944 were so certain that the Germans would adopt a defensive deployment that they did not even look for signals that Hitler might not take a fully rational approach to the problem of defending Germany, and hence missed the German buildup for the Battle of the Bulge.

At the time of the 1979 Iranian Revolution, the Shah deluded himself and others, including Iranians and foreign governments that a serious challenge to him and his regime was not growing. While embassy and intelligence officers got valid information, it wasn't enough to convince the U.S. government in Washington quickly enough in the face of previous history to the contrary.[11]

Individuals are frequently in error, but more often than not they realize their mistakes when matters begin to go wrong and events turn out differently than anticipated. There are cases, however, more numerous than one would hope, where persistence in error leads to folly because self-correcting mechanisms do not come into play for various reasons. An individual's ego is simply too tied up in a fixed position to permit change. His or her arrogance simply will not admit a wrong view, others' warnings are not heeded, and folly results.

Hard-line British statesmen and politicians in the pre-revolutionary and revolutionary period of the American Revolution—extending over twenty years—clearly fall into this category. From the time of the Stamp Acts forward, British prime ministers and lord chancellors were outraged at the colonies' reaction to governance from London without representation.

As matters grew worse and led to war, the willful blindness of Frederick Lord North and Lord George Germain toward the American colonies attitudes fostered colonial unity. The military defeats at Saratoga and Yorktown that brought down the British Government were the result of error persisted in to the point of folly. Statesmen on both sides of the Atlantic, most notably Edmund Burke in England and Benjamin Franklin in America (as well as most historians in the years since),

Benjamin Franklin
Source: Creator - Greuze, Jean-Baptiste, 1777, Wikipedia

believed that absent the stubborn, willful blindness of British statesmen, America would have maintained some sort of a political relationship with Great Britain.[12]

A similar phenomenon appeared during America's engagement in Vietnam from 1955-1975. Through four presidents, two from each party, America gradually escalated its involvement in Vietnam, fearing that if Vietnam fell, other South Asian states—"dominoes" would become communist as well. In the early years, from 1955 until 1965, an argument could be made in the Cold War context for the proportionality of this U.S. engagement to the goal sought—keeping Vietnam free.[13]

However, in 1966-68 when the subsequent steady march to a full commitment of half a million fighting men and women plus an overwhelming percentage of available American military and diplomatic resources to a small corner of the globe is assessed in a broader context, the term "folly" is certainly appropriate. It forced President Johnson out of the 1968 presidential race, alienated a generation of young American men and women, led to the conquest of South Vietnam by North Vietnam, and later created the domestic behavior that produced the Watergate scandal that promoted a deep distrust of government that has lingered and reemerged as a result of our invasion of Iraq in 2003. Interestingly enough, the "falling dominoes"—other nearby states going communist—did not occur when the U.S. left Saigon in 1975.

A generation of American statesmen, journalist David Halbertstam's "best and brightest," proved unable to reexamine their own faulty assumptions about America's ability to do whatever it wanted to without the solid, persevering support of the American people. Key leaders such as President Lyndon Johnson, Secretary of Defense Robert McNamara, Secretary of State Dean Rusk and others, including military leaders such as Commander, Military Assistance Command Vietnam, Gen. William Westmoreland, persisted in asserting and defending positions that an increasing number of political and diplomatic leaders came to believe were untenable. The parallel with our contemporary involvement in Iraq is unmistakable.

The parallel with the British leadership in respect to the American Revolution is also striking: arrogance and stubbornness persisted beyond the time when any rational calculation showed benefit—a simple unwillingness to back down. This latter trait of stubbornness seems more common the higher up one ascends the political and military ladder and leaves the "facts on the ground" behind, or submerged in more general reporting. This has also been the situation in Iraq in 2004-2006.

It ought to be a simple matter for leaders to learn from the past—but as many have suggested, and history has shown, such learning is more difficult than it appears. At the point where strong differences emerge, if wisdom were possible, leaders would reexamine their direction and a change of course would be considered. But it too seldom happens. Many believe President George W. Bush, Vice President Dick Cheney and former Defense Secretary Don Rumsfeld consistently exhibited this flaw.

Arrogance, false certainty, and persistence in beliefs that are not working—all produce inflexibility, set limits and reduce strategic possibilities for dealing with a problem. If reassessment does not occur, pursuit of the original mission, in the words of historian Barbara Tuchman, "enlarges the damages until it causes the fall of Troy, the [Protestant] defection from the Papacy, the loss of a trans-Atlantic empire, the classic humiliation in Vietnam."[14]

All the above are often magnified if the issues and players come from different cultures. In the Pearl Harbor case, Americans assumed the Japanese thought the same way they did about strategy and the relative hierarchy of goals. Few if any questioned the potential impact of the Roosevelt administration's embargo on shipments of strategic materials to Japan in July 1941. Instead of inducing compliance with American desires that Japan stop attacking its neighbors, it drove the Japanese warlords to consider attacking the U.S. rather than "submit" to the U.S. For the Japanese, "honor" was more important than "rationality," while the U.S. did not adequately appreciate the strength of the Japanese feeling that a showdown was unavoidable sooner or later.

Similar cross-cultural dissonances can be found elsewhere. British statesmen in London in the 1770s who pressed for a hard line against the colonies had little or no understanding of how the American experience had affected the colonists, and refused to listen to those who did. Likewise, American statesmen in the 1950s and 1960s knew little about Southeast Asia and less about guerrilla warfare, despite America's successful experience in the Philippines in 1950-54 as well as sixty years earlier. Similar issues have bedeviled America in U.S.-Iranian relations from the mid-1950s until now, and have been the centerpiece of our unhappy experience in Iraq since 2003. History will show us whether our learning curve can rise quickly enough to minimize the folly.

Pearl Harbor Attack—Battleship USS West Virginia took two aerial bombs (one dud) and seven torpedo hits; of the seven at least five were from aircraft and one from a midget submarine.
Source: Wikipedia

ORGANIZATIONAL COMPLEXITY

The problems noted above are multiplied many times when organizational issues are present. An excellent description of this can be found in Irving Janis' book, *Groupthink*. [15]

At Pearl Harbor, the major organizations in-volved—the separate Army and Navy commands in Hawaii—were very un-coordinated. Later, of course, after creation of the Defense Department in 1947, organization lines and links were clarified, and after the Goldwater-Nichols military reforms of the 1980s, unified theater commanders were put in place. The War Council in Washington (precursor of today's Joint Chiefs of Staff) did not even share similar views of the danger of the Japanese threat in late 1941. The Navy high command thought the Army had gone to a high state of readiness after a November 24 war alert from Washington, but neither bothered to check with the other; and the Navy assumed that Army radar and antiaircraft batteries were fully activated when this was not the case.

Janis and others suggest that ineffective organizational relations inhibit critical thinking about issues. As a consensus builds about an issue or a problem, dissenters are marginalized. The impact of this is to stifle doubts and discourage expression of alternative theses, let alone serious consideration of them. This phenomenon is known as "groupthink." Striving for consensus and cohesion overrides individual members' motivation to take a hard look at alternative courses of action. Without astute and balanced leadership, this easily affects intelligence organizations, which are more likely than other bureaucracies to generate dissenting information vis-à-vis other units. Where there is uncertainty about such information, individuals frequently resolve it in favor of the data supporting either their personal or organizational views.[16]

Examples of this abound: In the case of Vietnam, intelligence from the field was slanted and sometimes withheld if it did not agree with "the party line" expressed from Washington by senior leadership. Likewise, The "cooking" of American intelligence on Iraq in Washington has become a national scandal.

During the Iranian Revolution, evidence was often interpreted by U.S. organizations (State Defense, CIA) in ways which bolstered American policy of support for the Shah and minimized the danger to him and thus to America's position in Iran. In some cases, information was interpreted differently in the State Department from the way it was viewed within the CIA. The resulting organizational conflict was not resolved on at least two critical occasions,[17] when senior officials delayed timely action.

Saddam Hussein's logic that led Iraq to attack Kuwait in 1991, or to resist the U.S. to the point of destruction in 2003, suggest that in the former instance, he actually thought his army was capable of defeating any combination that could have been brought against him. After eight years of playing with the American and the UN inspectors over his WMD capability, he thought the U.S. would not attack because of the situation in the rest of the Middle East. Subsequent events have also shown major American blind spots in dealing with both Hussein and the Iranians.[18]

In each of these instances, however, the competition between intelligence agencies—military, CIA and State Department—worked to point out the problems. One of the problems with the 2005-6 reforms of the U.S. intelligence community—which centralized reporting—is that this unifying process will reduce the likelihood of competing interpretations working their way up to key decision makers. Serious consideration and attention should be given to maintaining different viewpoints and avoiding a one size fits all approach at the most senior levels.

In such a process of gathering intelligence through a large organization, management style becomes a serious issue. Given problems of misperception, bias and uncertainty, how do managers correct for these problems? Strategic planning units of some organizations are often given the role of exploring different concepts or providing independent analysis. At Pearl Harbor there was no such mechanism for bringing an alternative view to bear. During Vietnam the CIA differed frequently with Defense Department's intelligence estimates. In the end, but too late to save many lives, the CIA was proven right in its disagreement with Defense on such mundane matters as unit strength and the lack of significance of "body counts." The same sad tragedy is being replayed in Iraq currently as military estimates of insurgent numbers have proved sadly off the mark.

A judicial approach to intelligence strongly suggests that there should be competing avenues—each organization has its expertise in its own area—but that also requires senior officials (presidents, cabinet secretaries, agency heads and their senior advisors) to be skillful at moving issues to a head and making timely decisions. They must act with dispatch, with consideration of all options, and with appropriate humility and balance. Such is not always the case, but it should be the goal.

INTELLIGENCE AND DIPLOMACY

Since elements of the old OSS, precursor to the CIA, were integrated into the State Department just after World War II, the Secretary of State has had his/her own intelligence sub-unit, the Bureau of Intelligence and Research (INR), to process diplomatic intelligence and offer an alternative view to that offered by the department's geographic bureaus, as well as other agencies. Its record has been remarkably better than others, not least because it has a clear focus on overall diplomacy with minimal organizational distractions such as the CIA and the Defense Intelligence Agency have.

Organizational leaders have a considerable amount of responsibility for the effectiveness of their organizations in acquiring and assessing information. Obviously, one key element of this is to seek intelligent, well-balanced, curious people to work in an organization, and then to train them well. This has important implications for recruiting which are just beginning to be fully explored in corporate, government, and even university circles. Deep and detailed involvement of politicians in this organizational process is generally a negative factor. Intelligence work is not the place for the wayward third cousin seeking a job.

Recruitment and training of capable individuals of integrity alone is not enough—the organization itself must be structured to promote effective acquisition of information, timely in-depth analysis, and smooth integration of information into policy/decision-making processes. Beyond that, the organizational culture should be shaped to press top leadership to interact with their people so that flexibility and openness mark the cooperative process and dissent is tolerated.

In some instances in government, an individual provides the alternative view. A good example of this was the role played by George Ball on Vietnam in the early 1960s. As Deputy Secretary of State Ball sat in on key meetings in both the Kennedy and Johnson administration and presented the case for limiting involvement in Vietnam. President Johnson referred to him as his "in-house dove." Though the president seldom took Ball's advice, Ball was the principal channel by which at least some dissident information and assessment reached the President and other senior leaders.

A much sadder case was President George W. Bush's first Secretary of State, Colin Powell, who had an exceptional relationship with those in his own chain of command. Powell opposed the drift to war against Iraq in 2002-3, but at the president's request dutifully gave an important speech to the UN that set forth the case for war. The text turned out to be based on doctored intelligence. In the push toward war, his policy advice was rejected, and the much more pliant Condoleezza Rice later replaced him at the start of Bush's second term.

Secretary of State Colin Powell addressed the United Nations Security Council on February 5, 2003, presenting evidence of Iraq's continued defiance of UNSC Resolution 1441.
Source: www.state.gov

Sir Winston Leonard Spencer-Churchill
Source: Imperial War Museum Collections, created by the British Government

Powell dissented about going to war with Iraq, but the president and other cabinet officers did not accept his recommendation. He made the case that Iraq could be controlled by existing policy without going to war so the U.S. could concentrate on dealing with Al Qaeda and other terrorist problems. Powell opted not to take his dissent to the point of resigning, but there are many who believe that if he had done so the administration would not have been able to lead the country into the invasion of Iraq.

The question of leaving office if your views are not accepted is a moral and practical decision for each individual. Is it better for a member of the foreign policy team to "stay the course" or to resign? As Winston Churchill put it, "The most important decision in public service is the leaving of it," and the individual must work out the ethics of the situation in terms of the importance of the issue and his own beliefs. Jimmy Carter's Secretary of State, Cyrus Vance, resigned because Carter undertook the "hostage raid" in April 1979 to free American diplomats held in Tehran for over a year.[19] Vance felt the raid was a violation of international law, but his resignation was after the fact, not before.

In Powell's case, he remained on duty

Cyrus Vance, former Secretary of State
Source: Wikipedia

President Jimmy Carter
Source: Library of Congress

for nearly two years after his speech at the UN on WMDs, or until the end of the first Bush administration in January 2005. My own personal feeling as an ex-diplomat, is that Powell should have at least threatened to resign if the president pressed for war, since he might have be able to forestall a very bad decision for the country; in Vance's case, I feel he placed too much emphasis on a faulty legal point and would have served the president better by staying.

Whatever the decision by the individual dissenter, if dissent isn't at least carefully examined, leaders will not get the information they need to prevent either error or folly. Informal, personal norms of behavior will defeat formal organizational exhortations. There is a very fine line between building organizational support for a mission and discouraging dissent, which in itself may be a sign errors are being made or tolerated into folly.

Studying errors and follies suggests that a range of reasons—arrogance, rigidity and inflexibility, plus cross-cultural unawareness—are all part of the failure of human and organizational environments to deal successfully with their environments. But these are not the only problems. As environments change, adapting historical insights to the future requires a careful look at both the past and the future rather than rote application of past lessons learned. For intelligence, continual probing of potentially hostile situations is essential, but a greater understanding of human nature and historical circumstance and a willingness to forego ideological certainty are also important to prevent history from using us. There are seldom signals from heaven that we are about to embark on the wrong track.

Preparing for the Future

Rapid change is the hallmark of the current epoch, but we are more wary than our ancestors that change automatically means progress. Faster change increases the need for obtaining accurate, solid information about the evolving environment, be it in Iran or Antarctica. Those on the extremes who wish to abolish the intelligence agencies in effect want to throw the baby out with the bath water, and leave the country blind.

To the degree that intelligence collection implies less than acceptable morality, we would do well to heed another reminder of C.S. Lewis:

> The proper motto is not 'be good, sweet maid, and let who can be clever,' but 'Be good, sweet maid, and don't forget this involves being as clever as you can.' God is no fonder of intellectual slackers than any other slackers.[20]

It seems self-evident that the U.S. needs good intelligence. From General Motors to the Episcopal Church or the Boy Scouts, *all* organizations need good information, or "intelligence." This is increasingly true of foreign policy units where both intellectual integrity and cross-cultural astuteness need to be exceptionally well developed and exercised.

It mattered less when America had overwhelming power and a large group of allies who supported a series of mutually-agreed upon policies. Even then, information/intelligence needed to be well analyzed and shaped into an effective guide to action. Otherwise, these organizations would become increasingly marginalized by contemporary life, and alliances lose their effectiveness. The same is true of individuals, who draw on the work of such organizations to increase their knowledge.

But there are impediments. The growing speed of communication and faster flow of transportation requires us to know more about more things, more quickly. Ten years ago someone in the field of international relations could easily prepare a short talk on key international issues—the Cold War, trade issues, etc. Today, the structure of the world is less hierarchical, both politics and trade are more decentralized and complex. There are 192 members of the UN instead of the fifty that formed the organization in 1945, and the cultural mix is much greater as millions more individuals have joined the world conversation.

Cross-cultural problems have moved to the critical list. Thirty years ago many businessmen in Kentucky and surrounding states thought "foreign trade" meant selling across state lines. Today hundreds of small businessmen seek help from state and local specialists on trading abroad; New York bankers, in turn can not just focus on Europe or Japan, but have had to learn much about "the 'stans"—Tajikistan, Uzbekistan, Kazakhstan, etc., of Central Asia.

The emergence of the computer, e-mail and the Internet have greatly aided the expansion of our awareness, but these technologies also adversely affect intelligence and intelligence-gathering in another important way—by multiplying the volume of information available. This, in turn, complicates analysis by providing too much data. One almost feels obliged to check key Internet sites and join electronic exchange groups. Adequately searching becomes more important than it used to be, as well as more difficult to do. Among other results is a growing age gap—young people use the Internet more than their elders, and hence see the world somewhat differently. As one of my faculty colleagues put it a few years back, "a dizzying stream of unsifted information is the enemy of careful study."[21] We are clearly in a transition period when old methods are being challenged by the new.

Another implication of burgeoning information is the growing need to focus on what intelligence agencies call "all source" information. The distinction between classified and unclassified information has been breaking down for years. University of Kentucky Professor Vince Davis, a prominent student of governmental process, noted twenty-five years ago, "The

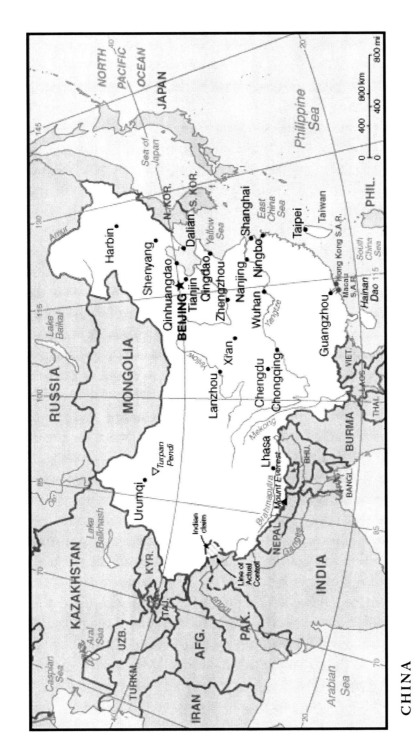

CHINA

Courtesy of The University of Texas Libraries. The University of Texas at Austin

invention of the Xerox machine seriously diluted our ability to keep secrets." The growing power of "secret-leakers," as opposed to "secret-keepers," beginning with the Pentagon papers in 1971, testifies to this.

The mushrooming of information also makes it even more difficult to enforce the traditional distinction between "secrets" and "mysteries." A secret is something that can be discovered, a fact that is not yet known—for example, the number of Iranian MIRV missiles, how many divisions Russia has on the Chinese border. A mystery is much more ephemeral—North Korea's intentions, Russia's plans, or why men and women bicker.

A certain consequence for policy/decision makers will be the need to deal with more probabilities and to develop action strategies to cope with the need for more rather then less certainty. The controversy over the use of biochemical weapons in the 1991 Gulf War exemplifies the difficulties inherent in the search for certainty as well as the difficulty of trying to draw secrets out of a mystery.

Sorting and searching, as well as developing an appropriate model or paradigm of what is relevant will take on increased importance for intelligence organizations—and for us all. For example, given limited resources, should the U.S. focus more on China, or on Russia? How much costly intelligence infrastructure should we devote to the states of the former Yugoslavia?

When one adds to this the problems of disinformation deliberately put forward by nations to mislead others, the problem again multiplies. Being taken in by a deception is an error; continuing to believe it as it unravels is folly. Two days after the Allies landed in Normandy in 1944, Hitler still thought the Allies' main thrust would come many miles away at Calais. The Allies had gone to great lengths to make him think that way, and the German Panzer divisions that might have driven our forces into the sea at the Normandy beaches never arrived there.

In the future, awareness of these possibilities must remain even closer to the analyst's consciousness. Setting parameters for assessment will become even more critical than it is now.

From governments to corporations, the need for counter-intuitive and probability analysis, the "what if . . ." scenario builders, will grow. Finding those who can do this work without excessively alienating their colleagues will be a real coup. More important, and perhaps more difficult, will be developing leaders who can live with and manage the resulting uncertainty, as well as a body politic that understands this.

**President
John F. Kennedy**
*Source: Wikipedia,
Cecil Stoughton,
White House*

Studying error and folly in history gives us a powerful sense of the "what ifs" in history and government: What if John Kennedy had lived? Would he have been more flexible and less rigid than Lyndon Johnson and withdrawn American troops from Vietnam, cutting American losses? Could a different group of British leaders have managed to mollify the colonists thereby creating a great trans-Atlantic federation in 1775? In the long run, would

**President
Lyndon B. Johnson**
*Source: Library of
Congress*

we have been better or worse off if any of those "what ifs" had happened?

While it is true that a "good" decision can turn out poorly without any reference to the way it was made, and "bad" decisions can turn out well despite the deficiencies of the process, in the long run most of us would bet on things done well to produce better results. To accomplish this, the most important quality an individual needs is a sense of humility and balance. Whether policy/decision maker, or citizen activist, this will greatly help him or her to avoid the arrogance of misplaced certainty and ideological fervor. It will also help defuse that cocksureness that leads those in all stations of life to ignore the warnings that would save them from both error and folly.

An awareness of the new and the complex is essential for effective common sense. Scholars, intelligence officers, political and business leaders—indeed, all of us—would do well to constantly bear in mind former Baltimore Oriole manager Earl Weaver's comment, "It's what you learn after you think you know everything that really counts."

---

[1] Tuchman, Barbara. *March of Folly.* (New York; Ballantine Books, 1984), chs. 1-2.

[2] Ameringer, Charles D. *U.S. Foreign Intelligence: The Secret Side of American History.* (Lexington: Lexington Books, 1990). An excellent and readable, swift review of U.S. Intelligence, including covert action, from the country's inception through the Reagan administration.

[3] Johnson, Loch. *America's Secret Power.* (Oxford: Oxford Univ. Press, 1989) pp. 3-56; and Jeffreys-Jones, Rhodri. *The CIA and American Democracy.* (New Haven Yale Univ. Press, 1989), Introduction and chs. 1 and 2.

[4] Breckinridge, Scott. *The CIA and U.S. Intelligence System.* (Boulder: Westview Press, 1986), Part 1.

[5] Richard Helms, in conversation with author, March 12, 1981.

[6] Richelson, Jeffrey. *The U.S. Intelligence Community.* (Boulder: Westview, 1995), p. 3.

[7] Breckinridge, op.cit., Parts 2 and 3; and Johnson, Loch K. and James J. Wirtz (eds.), *Strategic Intelligence: Windows into a Secret World.* (Los Angeles: Roxbury Publishing Co., 2004), Part VIII.

[8] Excellent examples and discussions of these points may be found in: Daugherty, William J. *Executive Secrets: Covert Action and the Presidency.* (Lexington, Univ. Press of Kentucky, 2004), chs. 1-3; Odom, William. *Fixing Intelligence.* (New Haven, Yale Univ. Press, 2006), chs. 7 and 9; Johnson. *America's Secret Power.* chs. 6-9.

[9] Daugherty, op. cit., Odom. *Fixing Intelligence.* chs. 7-9: Johnson and Wirtz. op. cit. chs. 17, 19, 21 and 28.

[10] Lewis, C.S. (Writing as N. W. Clerk). *A Grief Observed.* (Greenwich: The Seabury Press, 1963) p. 51. I am very indebted to Maj. Susan Hastings of the Virginia Military Institute Library for tracking down the source of this quotation after several senior scholars had failed.

[11] Stempel, John D. *Inside the Iranian Revolution.* (Bloomington: Indiana University Press, 1981), pp. 283-308; Selliktar, Ofira. *Failing the Crystal Ball Test* (Westport: Praeger, 2000), pp. 128-34.

[12] Carr, Caleb. "William Pitt the Elder and the Avoidance of the American Revolution," in Robert Cowley, (ed), *What Ifs? Of American History,* (New York: Berkley Books, 1999), pp. 17-42. Tuchman. op. cit., ch. 3.

[13] Ferguson, Niall. *Colossus: The Price of America's Empire.* (New York: The Penguin Press 2004), pp. 94-104; and Herring, George C. *America's Longest War: The United States and Vietnam, 1950-1975.* (New York: McGraw Hill, 1996), chs. 4 and 5.

[14] Tuchman. *March of Folly.* pp. 383.

[15] Janis, Irving. *Groupthink.* (New York: Houghton & Mifflin, 1982), chs. 1 and 4.

[16] Janis, Ibid., pp. 72.

[17] Stempel, op. cit., ch. 14; and Selliktar, op. cit., pp. 130-36

[18] Byman, Daniel, Kenneth Pollack and Gideon Rose. "The Rollback Fantasy, Foreign Affairs, January/February 1999, vol. 78, no. 1, pp. 24-41, and Risen, James. *State of War.* (New York: Free Press, 2006), pp. 1-10, and 219-23.

[19] Sick, Gary. *All Fall Down: America's Tragic encounter with Iran.* (London: I.B. Tauris, 1985), pp. 294-96 give a brief discussion of Vance's position. Powell has not commented on his leaving of the government.

[20] Lewis, C.S. *Mere Christianity* (New York: Macmillan, 1952) p. 75.

[21] Professor Margaret E.W. Jones, from an unpublished talk to the Modern Language Association, Savannah, 1996, p. 5.

CHAPTER 4
RELIGION & DIPLOMACY

If you love God and His world, you'd better know something about both.
—Mark Amstutz, Wheaton College

APPLYING COMMON SENSE TO A DISCUSSION OF RELIGION and diplomacy sounds like a thankless task. Belief systems, whether religious or secular ideologies, are often considered beyond reasoned discussion. In reality, however, nothing is more needed than a much more nuanced understanding of how the two relate, since they were separated in diplomatic practice and thought about five hundred years ago, and the world has changed significantly in the past sixty years.

Very early on, religion and diplomacy were closely linked, from the first sending of ambassadors representing sovereigns who had God's mandate in antiquity in the Middle East. Modern European diplomacy arose and became systematized in the seventeenth and eighteenth centuries precisely because the seventeenth century's thirty-years war had convinced both statesmen and clerics that humanity would collapse in Europe if religion and diplomacy were not separated. The 1648 Treaty of Westphalia stipulated that the ruler's religion would govern the land, and stopped religious infighting. Since that time, the exchange of diplomatic missions between countries has become the dominant form of communication between states and is referred to as "Westphalian Diplomacy."

Following 1648, wars of religion gave way to wars of national interest as nationalism emerged as the major political doctrine of state development. For about three hundred-four hundred years, conventional wisdom viewed religion as far less relevant to diplomacy in the modern secular, nationalist age. That is why most Americans and even Europeans tend to think of religion and diplomacy as two separate systems that seldom connect.

Beginning with the twentieth century rise of Jewish and Arab nationalism and the creation of the state of Israel in 1948 and accelerating with the Iranian Revolution (1979) and the end of the Cold War in 1989-91, religion has grown more central to international politics (and hence important to diplomacy). Religion has not replaced territorial issues and tribal rivalries, but it often intensifies them. There has been an increase in religious/ethnic/national conflict on all continents, which found expression in Harvard Professor Sam Huntington's "Clash of Civilizations" doctrine. He believes the coming twenty-first century conflicts will be between "civilizations"—Christian Europe versus Orthodox Eurasia, Muslims versus the West, etc. The rise of Islamic Jihadist terrorism over the past fifteen years and its expression on this continent on September 11, 2001 in the attack on the World Trade Center and the Pentagon brought the point home to all Americans as well as the rest of the world.[1] The link between religion and terrorism is a significant factor in the spread of violence in the past few years, and a crucial part of America's problems in Iraq and Afghanistan.[2]

That is one part of the story. Another is that far from being a purely negative factor, religion properly managed has played, and can play, an even more important positive role in diplomacy, and conflict resolution as well. In fact, it may be the only way to avoid a new millennium of religiously based wars. Religious values can strengthen diplomacy, and diplomacy provides tools for managing

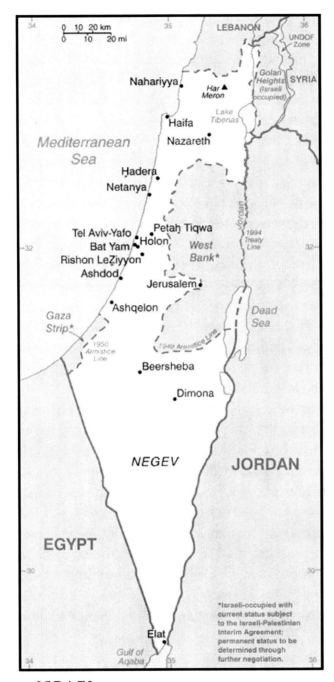

ISRAEL

Courtesy of The Universtiy of Texas Libraries, The University of Texas at Austin

and helping to resolve religious disagreements and ease religious conflicts. So religion is a double-edged sword—capable of being used for both good and ill. One of the biggest impediments to a positive outcome is the lack of real understanding about the linkages between religion and diplomacy.

There is a third view, held by some rationalists and atheists: religion is an impediment because it is irrational and we therefore must again get religion out of all policy areas if we are not to wind up with religious fanatics throwing nuclear weapons at each other because we can not "render our children incapable of killing themselves over their books." [3] It would be idyllic if we could do so, but even prominent atheist Sam Harris stops just short of saying that the *only* way to deal with fanatics is to meet violence straight on with violence. If one takes that tack, incineration is still more likely than peace. "Peace," however, can only be made by painstaking "diplomacy" which involves dealing with potentially hostile faiths in the most careful diplomatic ways, and using force only where unavoidable under direct threat.

For over twenty-five years, the international relations community has been wrestling with the renewed relationship between religion and diplomacy. While reviewing U.S. policy failures in Iran in 1978-9, scholars noted that U.S. and other policy/decision makers had systematically ignored the impact and influence of religion in Iran and elsewhere. They traced this to the pervasive belief in the U.S. and Europe that "modernization" had brought about increasing secularization of society. But it was becoming clear to those who studied the problem that religion was working its way back into other major political issues—not just in the Middle East, but also with the rise of related problems in the U.S. and elsewhere.

GLOBALIZATION

A religious component is part of the emerging discussion on globalization as well. The complex interaction of modern communications has led to the increasing interdependence of world commerce. The actual and potential dislocation this creates raises important value questions with significant religious components.[4]

For example, downward pressure on salaries in many areas in the U.S., and increasing lack of support for social or public good in what some describe as "millennial capitalism" threaten to dislocate or diminish the social protections upon which many disadvantaged now rely. This, coupled with a dramatic increase in social stress created by wholesale job transfers and economic relocation, creates fears that lead to unrest that turns toward religion as an escape. We see this in our own politics, as do the Europeans and the Japanese.

Particularly important is religion as both social and psychological base for choices that individuals and societies make.[5] Religious identity gives people the basis for what Richard Falk calls "humane global governance," and brings more weight into the struggle to protect and uplift the poor, rather than ordering society on purely economic values. It is in the common values of *all* religions that such elements as concern for the suffering, community solidarity, and respect for the children of God find their way into politics.

Religion is one of the main antidotes to the alienation created by aspects of modern capitalism and bureaucratization. That is why it is the driving force behind the "Shia revival," as scholar Vali Nasr describes it,[6] for those in the Middle East who see their societies coming apart. The Shia's thrust to prominence has now mobilized the Sunnis, who fear their influence is slipping. Their turmoil is upon us.

World systems theories, including Marxism, are inadequate explanatory elements because they focus exclusively on the material aspects of life. Such existing theories err because they exclude too much which affects life and leave no room for charismatic and spiritual elements that defy the best efforts of rational choice theorists. This is a problem with atheists and others like writer Sam Harris and other non-believers, as well as those professionals trying to turn political and international studies into a predictable universe by trying to pretend that we're all rational.[7] The answer for a large segment of mankind is not pure rationality at all; spiritual and charismatic elements are nearly always commingled with rational thought in all of us.

DIPLOMACY

Diplomacy has been connected to all religions since the first diplomats served as mediators between sovereigns who carried divine rights with them. American historians carry the story further by tracing the continuing influence of diplomacy and diplomats through the Westphalian period down to today.[8] A significant problem is that religion plays different roles at different times and places. Religious beliefs supply the underlying basis of meaning, which surfaces in domestic or international relations, sometimes on an intermittent basis (specific human rights issues), and sometimes as the central element of policy and action (the Iranian Revolution). A few cases will illustrate the point.

The Iranian Revolution placed religion at the forefront of Iranian society and policy-making on all issues. It totally changed Iran's government from a secularizing and modernizing monarchy to a theocratic, religiously fundamentalist state and society. The Khomeini revolution forced a new discussion of the importance of religion in international affairs, and is often considered the benchmark for religious involvement in politics.[9] It is the one country in the world where economic betterment takes second place to the quest for "salvation," as the ruling religious autocracy defines it.

Less well known is the role the Protestant Church played in the demise of the German Democratic Republic (GDR), when the

Federation of Evangelical churches provided space for discussion of politics and privately urged the regime toward a more open and progressive society. This culminated in church support of and protection for a series of demonstrations across East Germany that led to the fall of the Berlin Wall and the collapse of the GDR.[10]

Catholic and Protestant traditions have been well documented in diplomatic history and literature, forming the basis as they do for Western Westphalian diplomacy of the past four hundred years. Catholicism's impact today stems from tradition and doctrine reflected in the Catholic Church as an institution (the only one that has diplomatic representation, by the way), as a community, and as a system of thought. This includes the "Liberation Theology" founded in the 1970s in Latin America.

Protestantism has played a major role in Europe and especially the U.S. The Protestant rejection of hierarchy and focus on individual salvation became mingled with and driven by the American democratic experiment, and even today fuels American idealism and universal human rights aspirations.[11] Given the predominance of both traditions in Europe, it is certainly more accurate to consider the traditional Westphalian Balance of Power as a product of a Christian philosophy of restraint and balance, rather than merely a secular alternative to religious struggle.

Perhaps the most interesting evolution of this in the U.S. has been the resurgence of the evangelical tradition over the past fifty years. Evangelicals now substantially outnumber the "main line" liberal Protestants (Methodists, Presbyterians and Episcopalians). They are beginning to play a greater role in foreign policy and linking up with the other groups on issues like increased foreign assistance and humanitarian relief and support for Israel, if not for Zionism. The Evangelical tradition has a stronger background in missionary work, which gives the growing evangelical congregations more involvement in overseas activities than the other protestant denominations.[12]

The Eastern Orthodox Church has always played a significant role in the states where it was the dominant force—ten countries in Eastern Europe, all but one of whom (Greece) were communist for much of the past fifty years. In the 1990s, the newly-acquired independence of the Eastern European region, including Russia, has channeled Orthodox religious activity along nationalist lines, with criticism of free market economics and open political debate, which it sees also as a challenge to its monopoly.[13]

Islam and the West have been at odds since the time of the crusades, eight hundred-plus years ago. This has been for geopolitical as much as for religious reasons, though the two have reinforced each other throughout history. As this state of affairs became enmeshed with colonialism and the Arab nationalist response in the early twentieth century, religion became less important until the creation of Israel. Elsewhere in the Islamic world, Muslims clashed with Hindus as British India divided in 1947 into India and Pakistan.

**Hugo Grotius,
a philosopher,
Christian apologist,
playwright, and poet**
*Source: Wikipedia,
Portrait by Michiel Jansz
van Mierevelt, 1631*

Perhaps most important is that the Islamic diplomatic tradition antedates and is very similar to our own Westphalian system.[14] It should be; one of the principal Western creators of diplomacy, Hugo Grotius, based his own early work on Islamic diplomacy.[15]

Israel, particularly in the post-Holocaust world, became a unique and special beacon to Jews all over the world. This, plus the growing hostility of the Arabs, created the present geopolitical configuration in the Middle East. The Arab-Israeli Peace Process of the last forty-plus years has involved more diplomacy during that time than any other set of issues in the world.[16]

Less familiar are the roles of religion in Japan and China. Because of its particular geographic isolation, Japanese religion has had little effect on, or connection with, diplomacy in comparison to many other states where monotheistic traditions deeply affect ethical norms. Religion in Japan tends to function at familial and communal levels rather than at the level of universal beliefs in strongly held ethical imperatives or articles of faith. Only during the pre-World War II ascendancy of state Shintoism in Japan were patriotism and religion melded into a creed which was deeply impressed upon the populace. This ended after World War II, but in recent years both the academic and popular press in Japan warn against the possibility of a new turn toward religious nationalism. There is also tension between secularism, and fear of revived militarism fueled by religion. Religion in Japan, however, is still much less of an issue than in many other places.[17]

In China, the communist government that came to power in 1949 began eradicating religion from political and social life. Today, the Chinese Communist Party government energetically patrols religious activities and organizations such as the Falan Gong because it fears the growth of independent authority and civil institutions beyond its control, a common fear among authoritarian states. Nevertheless, religious views will play a role at the personal level and in the growing debate about personal rights. Christians in China—especially the Catholic Church—have been steadily increasing in numbers over the past ten years, but do not yet play a significant role. However, religion may yet turn out to be a greater factor in foreign politics, since Beijing is fending off penalties for violating religious and other human rights, and seeking to remove the Vatican mission from Taiwan.[18]

This resurgence of religion in foreign policy has been obvious not only in the Middle East, but in ethnic and religious struggles in Bosnia, Kosovo, and the emergence of a Slav/religious component to Russian foreign policy. This has been acerbated by the collapse of the bipolar U.S./Soviet Union structure at the end of the Cold War and the emergence of transnational problems such as global warming and HIV/AIDS—problems which no single nation can deal with alone.

FAITH ENTWINED WITH DIPLOMACY

The major change in diplomacy and international politics has been the creation of new states over the last five decades that brings the number of UN members to 192 (instead of the original fifty). Add to this the rapid increase in communications, transportation and the combination of non-governmental organizations (NGO's) with the power of the Internet, and the cacophony in both religion and diplomacy can be deafening. How does this manifest itself?

INDIVIDUAL BELIEF SYSTEMS

Most foreign policy officials, even in Iran, have scant grounding in religious/faith issues. That has not, until recently, been part of the dialog in Washington, London or Tokyo. But it isn't just top bureaucrats or the politicians who have to truly understand faith/religious issues. All levels of policy/decision-makers have to have some idea of what's going on, so that common sense on these issues can make sense up and down the chain.

Individual beliefs of key players affect not only their perceptions of issues, but also what they do. Studies of American presidents and statesmen have shown this: Wilson's Presbyterian sternness and moralism; Dulles' and Reagan's religious views about the evil of the Soviet Union; and President George W. Bush's faith and its link to his policies have come under critical attention since the beginning of the move toward war in Iraq.

Beyond governments, a number of people of faith are now in fact practicing something called faith-based diplomacy, which involves conflict resolution missions in sensitive areas. Such efforts have taken place in Africa, notably the Sudan, Rwanda, and

Burundi, and in Asia with Hindu-Muslim conflicts in India and Indonesia. This is something new, and has been very helpful in defusing some major conflicts.[19] It is not yet fully part of our public awareness, and the links between it and official governmental diplomacy are very slender. Such efforts do open ways for greater religious and secular collaboration, which is occurring now in the Middle East.[20]

NATIONAL AND INTERNATIONAL BELIEF SYSTEMS

These include philosophies, intellectual currents, and beliefs that contribute to national and organizational views. They can be distinguished from individual attitudes, but obviously influence them. The secularist view of modernization is one such position; The Western idea of continual upward progress and the opposing image of the cyclical view of history—that events repeat themselves over the years and centuries—are others. Islamic radical views, which see the West as corrupt, and modernizing governments as tools of Satan, are important political as well as religious ideas. Contained in this body of thought is a carefully worked out philosophy of terrorism, which is substantially at odds with Western as well as much Islamic tradition.[21]

Religion has helped shape America's values since its earliest days when Americans saw the U.S. as the "New Jerusalem," the "City Upon a Hill" where people could work out their destinies free of old restraints—and as a "beacon on the hill" for others. Belief in a divine creator, if not in a state religion, suffused our political life—and still does despite increasing twentieth century secularization. In practical foreign policy terms, missionaries were engaging in their own forms of "diplomacy" before the U.S. even had a diplomatic service, and missionaries outnumbered American diplomats abroad until well into the 1960s. This unique American experience also includes relative freedom from the pain and disasters of war. With the exception of our own revolution in 1776, and the terrible violence of our Civil War, 1861-1865, our social order has been remarkably free of the worst impact of war, unlike Europe and Asia.

History may be coming full circle—over the past ten years, the privatization of some aspects of foreign policy has led to increasingly prominent roles for church-connected relief agencies such as the Catholic Relief Service, Jewish relief efforts, the American Friends Service Committee, World Vision, and the Episcopal Presiding Bishop's Relief and Development Fund, among others.

In the past decade, American religious evangelicalism (in alliance with some fundamentalists) has had greater visibility in overseas-related activities.[22] The creation in 1999 of an Office of Religious Freedom in the State Department as a result of the Wolfe-Specter Bill in response to the Christian Right has been an interesting experiment. It has drawn more attention to religion and diplomacy, but stimulated at least one "get lost" reaction on the part of a major government, India, which refused to receive our Ambassador of Religious Freedom when he sought to visit that country. They said, in effect, that it was none of his business, and India rejects "any intrusive exercise into how we conduct our affairs."[23]

SPECIAL ISSUES RELIGION POSES FOR STATECRAFT

... Religion is an intractable force that can be unresponsive to all the instrumentalities of state power, let alone the instrumentalities of foreign policy.

—Edward Luttwak

Tapping religious fervor may be a good way to build support in a conflict, or create a slogan for battle—but it also ties statesmens' hands when it comes to negotiating a settlement. Continuing peace negotiations in Northern Ireland and the Middle East underline the point. Diplomats generally deal with power and conflict—their stock in trade is persuasion, bargaining and deals. Religious motivations are transcendent and unpredictable, often stimulated by prophetic visions—the Mandate of Heaven, the Word of the Prophet.[24] Those who act in their name seek victory, historical vindication, and have a deeply hostile view of the "others-as-enemy." In common sense terms, their enmity runs far deeper than most international politics.

This is not conducive to settlements and more likely to lead to Armageddons. It can be very dangerous indeed when dealing with nuclear issues or other weapons of mass destruction. Indeed, during the Cold War, the Soviets were very concerned about American fundamentalism and what they saw as its potential for seeking Armageddon in crisis situations. The fact that few scholars and perhaps even fewer statesmen, theologians or media folk are very knowledgeable in both fields is a scary proposition. Those who know statecraft often admit they are beginners in spiritual matters, while few theologians would claim experience in diplomacy or the political scramble. Where is Cardinal Richelieu (seventeenth century Catholic prelate and also French Foreign Minister) when we need him?

The interplay between religion and politics/diplomacy is subtle and complex. Getting religious fervor behind a political struggle may act as a force multiplier—as in Northern Ireland, Bosnia or Kosovo—but it can also bring the machinery of conflict resolution to a halt. Worse, it can even leave societies in ruins as in Lebanon, 1975-1990 and in the summer of 2006—or Algeria, Armenia and Azerbaijan today.

Used rightly—and no one is exactly certain how to make this interplay work all the time—it is capable of helping to resolve conflicts, focus peoples' as well as negotiators' minds toward peace, and to help deal with some of the more negative aspects of globalization. On the other hand, historians note the paradox that true believers have been responsible for some of the most sublime as well as the most sordid events in history.

Prospects of nuclear, chemical or biological terrors have not been banished, and may even be growing, as Iran and North Korea illustrate. The increasing weakness of the social order in so many places, spurred on by disease and poverty, suggests that complacency and withdrawal are inappropriate responses to international questions on either secular foreign policy or religious grounds. Religiously motivated terrorism decisively underlines the point, as the next chapter notes.

If the coming age is one of reforming and reshaping values, diplomacy will be called into the service of dealing with such problems. Preventive diplomacy—heading off conflict and disaster before they arrive—and effective conflict resolution abilities are becoming at least as important as classical geostrategic, economic and political-military skills. The logistics and costs of relief efforts, refugee politics and assistance move us away from violence. Religious people of all faiths have traditionally focused their efforts in this direction, and even today accelerate these activities.

Perhaps more important, we must move past the rigid traditional political analysis of the hard-core realist school of international politics, whose focus on power ignores so much of what else happens in the world. The arguments on both sides—often called the realist-idealist debate—have too often created a schism that has made gradual organic change difficult. Some amelioration of this divide is necessary in any case for the more critical task of getting religious thinkers and international relations scholars to talk constructively with each other, and to deal with issues of peace, pacifism and conditions for the moral use of force.

Both religion and diplomacy need to get beyond the trivializing attitude represented by the rationalist who said "Going to war over religion is basically killing each other to see who's got the better imaginary friend."[25] Religious differences have been a highly divisive factor of conflicts in Bosnia, Northern Ireland, Chechnya, Southeast Asia, and the Middle East. They not only cause such conflicts, but also are a contributing, often decisive factor in their continuance. There, religions' involvement is plain. However, one almost has to read between the lines to discover that large church organizations were also involved in recent serious peacemaking efforts in several instances, most notably in the Sudan, Burundi and Rwanda.[26]

Perceptive theologians even recognize that religion can have its dark side. Serious efforts have been made to ease this within most faiths in recent years, as well as some efforts between faiths. Progress may seem less than it is because it has also occurred at a time when religious conflict has been growing, often in connection with ethnic disturbances. Such effective interaction will be crucial to eventually resolving Western difficulties with the Muslim world.

One of the key issues is how we view "others." Is the "other" a "child of God," or the "evil enemy?" History illustrates that horrors have been perpetrated by all faiths when they have tilted toward the dark side of "otherness." Christianity has much to answer for with respect to the Crusades and the Inquisition. Muslims, Hindus and Buddhists all have their historical tragedies as well. The emergence of radical extremisms in political life from all faiths has increased concern on this point.

On the other hand, religious beliefs underlying foreign policies have also had very positive effects in history as well. While it was based as much on perceptive politics as directly upon religion, the Allied willingness to "forgive" Japan and Germany at the end of World War II laid the basis for over sixty years (and counting) of major peace.[27] Contrast this with the focus on the vengefully draconian peace imposed upon Germany in 1919-20, which led to the economic collapse of Europe, the rise of Hitler, and to the second World War.

We take it for granted that the Cold War ended peacefully, but such historic confrontations have not always ended as benignly— Athens vs. Sparta and Rome vs. Carthage, for example. It can be fairly argued that the absence of a Western revenge-motivated foreign policy, coupled with the open hand held out to Russia and the other states of the ex-Soviet Union, made possible the peaceful dissolution of the "evil empire," rather that a desperate struggle which could have precipitated a nuclear conflict. The West's Judeo-Christian tradition was an important factor in the emergence of such a policy.

On the other hand, the double-edged nature of religion contributed to the severe peace imposed upon the losers in World War I, and helped turn the American Civil War into a bloody four-year battle to exhaustion. Today, it is a driving force of the terrorist threat to our society.

The idea of bringing religions together is not new, just newly important. Fr. Bede Griffiths, the English Benedictine who ran an ashram in India for thirty years until his death in 1993, spoke of a "Perennial Philosophy" which is present in all religions. He asserted that the world's religious traditions are interrelated, and that each has its own insights as well as its own unhelpful customs.[28]

Commenting just before his death, Father Bede said, "The deeper you go, the more all religions are alike." Such common ground as respect for the individual soul, certain (but not all!) moral prohibitions and exhortations, and respect for God underlie all religious efforts to some degree. They provide a basic set of values for diplomacy as well. As a basis for planetary coexistence, Griffiths' work provides an excellent starting point, particularly for un-demonizing the "other" as well as exploring bases of common interest and agreement.

In fact, much practical work has already been done in this area across religious lines, particularly among Middle Eastern groups. Much of this has been the basis for such peace as we have had. Research has shown that certain moral and social characteristics of religious communities uniquely equip them to promote religious peace.

Interfaith dialog is often aimed at an ecumenical outcome, bringing churches together. But it is not a sure thing—it can water down doctrine to the point that it looses the sacred authority behind it, as the World Council of Churches tends to do.[29] As Gandhi once noted, "I don't want you to become a Hindu, I want you to be a good Christian."

CONTEMPORARY WORLD VIEWS

If diplomats, politicians, and many citizens know little about religion, many of those deeply occupied with religion are similarly uninformed about the world of politics.

One's views determine how one is likely to apply one's faith and whether and how one is likely to attempt, and succeed at, diplomacy. In the U.S. and elsewhere, Christians have had particular difficulty coming to reasonable grips with the role of force in international affairs and this has distanced them from mainstream public understanding. Following Christ's admonition, "blessed are the peacemakers," Christian pacifists have either sought to exclude force completely from international affairs or taken a perfectionist view of ethics which leads to a fanaticism that distances them from reality.[30] Example of this can be found in most other religions as well.

For example, at the onset of the 1991 Gulf War, both U.S. national Catholic and Protestant leadership strayed into ideological fields, some distance from general opinion in their vocal opposition to any use of force against Iraq. However, most practicing Christians would be, and were, comfortable with the

Persian Gulf War
Source: Wikipedia

Christian realism espoused by Reinhold Niebuhr and the contextualist approach to statecraft/force which has generally held sway over contemporary Western statesmen.

The Niebuhrian view of Christian realist ethics (found best in his two books, *Christian Realism and Political Problems* and *The Irony of American History*) may simply and very roughly be described as "If you argue for a given position, you must be prepared to argue for, or at least accept, the likely consequences." If you don't want to fight, are you willing to suffer the consequences of loosing to Nazis, communists or Al Qaeda? Committed pacifists have often dealt naively and inadequately with the necessary use of force in support of justice.

JUST WAR AND JUST PEACE

High on the list of issues of reconnecting religion, diplomacy and international relations in a positive and helpful way will be the ancient doctrines of "just war" and "just peace," and in the Islamic world, the question of *Jihad*. The concept of "just war" goes all the way back to Thomas Aquinas in the thirteenth century, but it really began to be taken seriously and practically by monarchs, politicians, diplomats and military men as the Thirty Years War ended in 1648. As nationalism grew more virulent in the eighteenth and nineteenth centuries, "just war" took a back seat to power politics and political realism. "Might makes right" became the order of the day in great power politics, interrupted by Woodrow Wilson's vision of collective security and international responsibility. The fascist dictatorships of the following years revived the might/right doctrine in the 1930s, but after World War II and in the crucible of the Cold War, issues of morality returned.

President Thomas Woodrow Wilson

Source: Wikipedia, Pach Brothers Portrait Photograph Collection

In the 1970s and '80s, spurred on by considerations of Vietnam, a new consensus emerged on older principles. The basic tenets of Just War are these:

1. **Just Cause**—Is there a real or certain danger that can only be confronted by war or threat of war? Several objectives: protect against conquest of independent state (Kuwait), deter and repel aggression, safeguard human rights, prevent genocide, assure adequate and affordable energy supplies, advance a new international order, or overthrow a hostile dictator.

2. **Competent authority**—In the U.S., the issue is between the president and congress. Who can/should get us into war?

3. **Right intention**—Are the given reasons actual ones and moral ones?

4. **Last resort**—Have all peaceful alternatives been fully pursued. Example: could the international economic and political pressure on Iraq bring about a just solution over time without resort to violence?

5. **Just Peace**—Is the action committed to achieving a just peace?

There is a dispute about this: If the other issues are met, is it better to use force when you should rather than when you must? Former Secretary of State George Shultz noted "last" meant "no other" resort, and by that time the level of force and risk involved may be too great to do what you should have done when you could have done it.

    6. Probability of success—Is the prospect of success sufficiently clear to justify the human and other costs of military action?

    7. Proportionality—Are the damages to be inflicted and the costs incurred by war proportionate to the objectives to be achieved by taking up arms? Are the expressed values at stake so important that they justify resorting to the use of force?[31]

American diplomacy has not made a fetish of adherence to the details of "just war," but it has always argued that the U.S. was right in what it did, and argued it was "just." Even where one may disagree with a specific action, the list of principles can be a solid common sense guide to what actions should justifiably and reasonably explored in the decision to employ force.

For example, the U.S. decision to invade Grenada in 1983 turned on the danger to American citizens and the Grenada government's buildup of weapons for use by Latin rebel groups. In the decision to fight Iraq in 1991 common sense American opinion favored the views that this was defense against aggression as well as protecting the world oil supply.

The controversy over going to war against Iraq in 2003 was, interestingly enough, triggered by the president's own secretary of state. Colin Powell argued within the administration that it was unnecessary to invade to achieve our most important objectives, and to attack Iraq would provoke greater conflict which would defeat our basic objective (thus violating points one, three and four of the "just war" doctrine). Others argued that our preparation was inadequate for the greater task, and hence violated points six and seven as well. The majority view over time has come to be that the 2003 conflict against Iraq does not meet "just war" criteria.

The application of "just war" theory to terrorism will be discussed in the next chapter, but the theory itself traditionally focused on state-to-state relations. However, another development arose out of the question of when it is just to fight, namely what circumstances create a "just peace?" Liberation theologists justified resort to war and rebellion by appeals to social injustice and evil conditions in their societies. What then, would a "just peace" look like?

In the early 1990s, a combined team of theologians and scholars took a renewed look at earlier doctrines of "just war" and Just Peace. Theologian Glen Stassen summarized their work in *Just Peacemaking: Ten Practices for Abolishing War.*[32]

They undertook this effort to clarify the choices for all faiths in an era when "humanitarian interventions" had become a primary concern. Christians and others have led the way in support of peacemaking as an activity, and the application of conflict resolution techniques to try and avoid violence.

Stassen's list of ten practices for abolishing war:

PEACEMAKING INITIATIVES
1. **Support nonviolent direct action**—boycotts, strikes, marches, civil disobedience, public disclosure, accompaniment and safe space;

2. **Take independent initiatives to reduce threats**—decrease threat, stand-alone, works best—if reciprocated can continue (arms reduction);

3. **Use Cooperative Conflict Resolution (CCR)**—active co-working of parties to conflict. Arab Israeli peace example; Trust in Yugoslavia. Issues: Cultural Barriers, degree of

damage/pain, problems of scale, power inequities. Need to alter perceived reality in irreducible conflict;

4. **Acknowledge responsibility for conflict and injustice and seek repentance and forgiveness**—Transcend own pride, interests empathy, repentance and forgiveness. U.S. acknowledge ills—Japanese, Axis acceptance of responsibility. Iran hostage statement.

JUSTICE

5. **Advance Democracy, Human Rights, Religious liberty**—Post-Cold War political liberalization, economic interdependence, influence of international law/ organization. Spreading Zones of Peace. Special problems of ethnic conflict.

6. **Foster just and sustainable economic development**— Environmentally constructive development. Development to promote end of poverty, measure of justice. Injustice in debt structure, conflicts in needs, resources (oil, water). Sustainability versus greed.

LOVE AND COMMUNITY

7. **Work with emerging cooperative forces in the international system**—International System is *both* cooperative *and* conflictual. Tension among governmental goals. Trend in system toward decline in utility of war, rise of trading, dramatic increase in volume, density of international exchanges, increase in democracy. "Free rider" problem in concerted action—all want benefits, few are willing to pay.

8. **Strengthen UN and international efforts for cooperation and human rights**—Collective action.

Peace keeping, Peace building and peace enforcement—
even if sovereign rights are abridged in egregious cases.

9. **Reduce offensive weapons and weapons trade**—Nuclear,
   land mines. Code of conduct for conventional transfers.

10. **Encourage Grassroots peacemaking groups and voluntary association**—Network of NGO's, build sense of
    community among People, not just leaders.[33]

Religiously motivated scholars, more than secular thinkers,
have pushed the notion of "justice" into the equation for calculating
the just use of force. George Weigel offers a classic Christian
formulation of "true peace" as:

> Rightly ordered and dynamic political community
> in and among nations, in which legal and political
> institutions provide effective means for resolving
> the inevitable conflicts that will define public life
> until the End of Time.[34]

This would be familiar and acceptable to mainline Islamic
thought as well as to Christians.

Similarly, Christian and most other faiths' concern for the
poor and desire to build community relate very closely to the issue
of combating chaos and building a just world order. Christians
accept (to varying degrees, of course) John Donne's famous
statement, "ask not for whom the bells toll; they toll for thee." This
concern has supplied one of the strongest motives for Western
assistance to those in need over the past forty years. This, despite
the fact that "Christian" America has sunk to the bottom of the list
of industrialized countries in terms of *per capita* governmental
foreign assistance. (When our private and religious financial aid
is counted, we move up the list a bit.)

What is striking about the "ten practices" Stassen and his colleagues have developed is that they are keyed to the types of issues politicians and diplomats have to face. In some cases, they provide a model for informal and NGO diplomacy practiced by non-governmental diplomats.[35] Common sense suggests that if one is really interested in peace, one should look to providing development for the poor, and this should take greater priority in our foreign policy. Frequently our churches have been better stewards of this process than our government.

Impact of New Religion/Diplomacy Ties

Ambassadors and others are beginning to integrate some of the value shifts brought about by a greater emphasis on religion into their view of what constitutes their work. Properly used, citizen diplomacy and faith-based diplomacy can supplement or reinforce traditional diplomacy—or even take over some tasks, as religious and private groups' work in Africa over the past two decades has suggested.

Those "amateurs" engaged in such diplomacy, however, could learn a great deal from diplomatic professionals in the process, as some have. There are even greater possibilities of valuable coordination and support if common sense understanding and collaboration can replace prejudices on both sides. Each side has what the other needs.

On the political side, a good, basic common sense understanding of how religion interacts with politics should also produce a policy approach that pulls religious moderates and natural allies along with us. The more we interact with others and harmonize our basic values, the more likely we are to build support throughout the world.

The disastrous slide in U.S. popularity over the past four years is ironic for a country that has promoted religious freedom. For example, in mid-2001, before the 9/11 boost, virtually all countries except North Korea showed well above 50 percent approval of

America; afterward, 80 and 90 percent favorable ratings were common for about a year. By February 2005, the widely respected PIPA program showed only three of twenty-two countries surveyed showing over 50 percent, the highest of which was Iran, of all places, with a 69 percent favorable rating.

America's "either with us or against us" politics of the post-9/11 period promoted the clash of civilizations that Huntington warned about. Without a different tack—the need to build community by stressing the basic harmony between religions on key points more true to our own values, we will find far fewer allies on all issues—but especially against Islamic terrorists—than we need in those parts of the world which do not share our own faith. There is no point to rearranging the deck chairs on the *Titanic* when we need to learn how to melt the icebergs. A key element in doing that will be to

NORTH KOREA

Courtesy of The Universtiy of Texas Libraries, The University of Texas at Austin

understand the interaction between religion and terrorism, in order to manage our policy judgments more effectively as well.

---

[1] Elements of this chapter have been adapted from my Paul Stauffer Lecture at the Lexington Theological Seminary, October 18, 2005, "Religion and Diplomacy," subsequently published in the Lexington Theological Quarterly, vol. 40, no. 3, Fall 2005, pp. 153-72.

[2] Harris, Sam. *The End of Faith.* (New York: W.W. Norton, 2005). pp. 48-49; see also his *Letter to a Christian Nation* (New York: Alfred A. Knopf, 2006), pp. 87-91.

[3] Anonymous. *Imperial Hubris: Why the West is Loosing the War on Terror.* (Washington: Brassey's Inc, 2004).

[4] Friedman, Thomas L. *The World is Flat.* (New York: Farrar Straus and Giroux, 2005), pp. 1-40, and 198-205.

5 Freidman, Thomas L. *The Lexus and the Olive Tree.* (Farrar Straus Giroux, 1999), ch. 1 and conclusion; Mazur, Jay. "Labor's new Internationalism," *Foreign Affairs,* January/February 2000, vol. 79, no. 1, pp. 79-93; Falk, Richard. "The Religious Foundations of Humane Global Governance," paper prepared for Religion and World Order symposium, Maryknoll, N.Y., May 1997; and Friedman, op. cit.

[6] Nasr, Vali. *The Shia Revival: How Conflicts within Islam Will Shape the Future.* (New York, W.W. Norton, 2006), chs. 6 and 9.

[7] Wuthnow, Robert. "Understanding Religion and Politics," Daedalus, Summer 1991, pp. 1-20; Easterbrook, Gregg. "Science and God: A Warming Trend?" SCIENCE, vol. 277, August 13, 1997, pp. 890-3.

[8] Der Derian, James. *On Diplomacy* (Cambridge, MA: Blackwell, 1987), chs. 1-4; Walter A. McDougall, "Religion in Diplomatic History, in <u>American Diplomacy</u>, an Internet magazine found at: John D. www.unc.edu/depts/diplomat/amdipl_12/mcdougall_rel.html

[9] Stempel, John D. *Inside the Iranian Revolution.* (Bloomington, IN: Indiana University Press, 1981), pp. 309-19.

[10] Pieratt-Seeley, Carey. "The Development of the Public Sphere Within the Protestant Church in the German Democratic Republic, 1950-89," paper presented at the International Studies Association Southern Regional meeting, Lexington, KY, November 12-14, 1999 (adapted from her Duke University PhD dissertation); Johnston, *Religion and Statecraft,* op cit., ch. 7.

[11] Langan, John. "The Catholic Vision of World Affairs," *ORBIS*, Spring 1998, Vol. 42, no. 2, pp. 241-62; and Kurth, James Kurth. "The Protestant Deformation and American Foreign Policy," *ORBIS*, op. cit., pp. 221-40.

[12] Mead, Walter Russell. "God's Country?" *Foreign Affairs*, September/October 2006, vol. 85, no. 5, pp. 24-43.

[13] Radu, Michael. "The Burden of Eastern Orthodoxy," *ORBIS*, op. cit., pp. 283-300.

[14] Kelsay John. *Islam and War: A Study in Comparative Ethics*. (Louisville, KY: Westminster/John Knox Press, 1993), pp. 1-7 and ch. 12.

[15] Grotius, Hugo and A.C. Campbell. *The Rights of War and Peace: Including the Law of Nature and Nations*. (New York: M.W. Dunne, 1901).

[16] Sicherman, Harvey. "Judaism and the World: The Holy and the Profane," ORBIS, op. cit., pp. 195-220; Bernard Lewis powerfully recounts this process in his two books—*What Went Wrong? Western Impact and Middle Eastern Response*. (Oxford, Oxford Univ. Press, 20020; and *The Crisis of Islam: Holy War and Holy Terror*. (New York: The Modern Library, 2003).

[17] Hurst, G. Cameron, III, "The Enigmatic Japanese Spirit," *ORBIS*, op. cit., pp. 301-24.

[18] Waldron, Arthur. "Religious Revivals in Communist China," *ORBIS*, op. cit., pp. 325-35.

[19] Johnstone, Douglas and Cynthia Sampson. *Religion: The Missing Dimension of Statecraft* (Oxford, Oxford Univ. Press, 2004), Introduction.

[20] Nasr, op. cit., especially pp. 119-23.

[21] Esposito, John L. "Iran, Islam and Democracy" *The Economist*, op. cit.; *The Islamic Threat: Myth or Reality?* rev. ed. (Oxford, 1995.)

[22] Ribuffe, Leo. "Religion and American Foreign Policy: The Story of a Complex Relationship," *National Interest*, Summer 1998, no. 52, pp. 37-50; and Martin, William. "The Christian Right and American Foreign Policy," *Foreign Policy*, Spring 1999, pp. 66-81.

[23] "U.S. Envoy on Faith Not Welcome," Pioneer News Service, New Delhi, September 13, 1999. An Indian Foreign Ministry spokesman said there was "no plan or intention to invite such an official or to engage in discussion," and added, "The Government and people of India reject any intrusive exercise into how we conduct our affairs."

[24] McDougall, op. cit., p. 2.

[25] Comment heard from the floor at an interfaith discussion, January 25, 2006.

[26] Crocker, Chester A., Fen Osler-Hampson, et. al. (eds), *Herding Cats: Multiparty Mediation in a Complex World.* (Washington: U.S. Institute of Peace, 1999).

[27] See, for example, Schriver, Donald. *An Ethic for Enemies: Forgiveness in Politics.* (New York: Oxford University Press, 1995).

[28] Griffiths, Bede. *A New Vision of Reality: Western Science, Eastern Mysticism, and Christian Faith.* (Templegate Press, 1989), ch. 12.

[29] McDougall, op. cit., Part II, p. 4.

[30] Rasmussen, Larry (ed.) *Reinhold Niebuhr: Theologian of Public Life.* (Minneapolis, MN: Fortress Press, 1991) pp. 230-53.

[31] List compiled by the author from several sources, including Weigel, op. cit., pp. 59-61 and 79-86; and Ramsey, Paul. *The Just War: Force and Political Responsibility.* (Boulder, CO: Rowman & Littlefield Publishers, 1983), chs 1, 9 and 10.

[32] Stassen, Glen. *"Just Peacemaking" Ten Practices for Abolishing War.* (San Francisco: The Pilgrim Press, 1998). For summary, see introduction.

[33] Ibid, condensed from chapter concepts.

[34] Weigel, George. *Just War and the Gulf War.* p. 85.

[35] "New Emissaries and No Emissaries: The Representation of New Voices in Global Politics," unpublished paper by Richard Langhorne for August 28-30, 2000 CISS/ISA Conference, Washington, D.C.

CHAPTER 5

TERRORISM & INSURGENCY

One man's terrorist is another man's Freedom Fighter.
                                        —Col. Edwin Lansdale

MANY YOUNGER AMERICANS THINK OF TERRORISM AS beginning with the destruction of the World Trade Center in New York on September 11, 2001. However, the problem has been around for two or three thousand years, perhaps longer. Terror attacks have been the weapon of choice for the weak against the powerful from biblical days to the present. Suicide terrorism is not that new either.

Terrorism isn't simply killing, though the modern concept came into use during the French revolution. As used today, it has a political aim and motive. It is violent— or threatens violence if its aims are not met. It is designed to have a far-reaching impact beyond the immediate victim or target. Terrorism is conducted either by an "organization

View of the Statue of Liberty as seen from the water on the morning of September 11, 2001, with the World Trade Center towers in the New York City Skyline.
Source: National Park Service

with an identifiable chain of command or a conspiratorial cell structure . . . of individuals directly motivated or inspired by the ideological aim or example of some existent terrorist movement and/or its leaders."[1]

Insurgencies and guerrilla warfare are often equated with terrorism, but go beyond it in terms of organization and mission. Guerrillas are larger groups of individuals who carry out hit and run raids and exercise control over some territory. Insurgents go beyond the idea of hit-and-run attacks, mobilizing others in support of taking control of particular territory. In this, they conduct psychological warfare and seek to build political support.[2]

In our own history, terrorism, guerrillas and insurgencies have been used by the U.S. and against us. The thirteen colonies used all three methods against the British in their struggle for independence. During the American Civil War of 1861-65, both sides used all three forms at various times. Hence the wry validity of Colonel Lansdale's quote at the beginning of the chapter. Such fighting is good for you, but bad when others use it against you.

Indian attacks against the early colonists were an important part of frontier history until late in the nineteenth century, and involved both terror attacks and guerrilla violence. During the Civil war, terrorism blended into guerrilla violence with Morgan's Raiders and Quantrell's Raiders, among others, not quite reaching the insurgency level. Later, nineteenth and early twentieth century anarchist movements were responsible for several political assassinations and attacks.

Homegrown terrorist/insurgent movements such as the Ku Klux Klan, and more recently the local militia movements keep this strain of activity alive, as the Oklahoma City bombings of a decade ago and the emergence of private militias in recent years attest.[3]

Abroad, contemporary terrorism began with the rise of Middle Eastern movements. A spate of terrorist activities and plane hijackings in the late 1960s and early 1970s brought terrorist kidnappings to the fore in Europe. Interestingly enough, the Europeans and the Japanese did not call for a "war" against terror. They joined with us and others to make eradication of the problem the prime effort of international police, intelligence and even some paramilitary forces. Within a few years the problem subsided, with little damage to the democratic systems of the countries involved.[4]

Contemporary international terrorist problems have their origins in the political events of the Middle East and Southeast Asia as they evolved from World War II to the present. In the process, terror again became involved in fundamental ways with religious issues, particularly after the end of the Cold War, when the Middle East saw the evolution of several Islamicist political movements.

The creation and rise of the state of Israel in the late 1940s provoked a reaction from the Arab nationalist movement and gradually led to heightened Arab nationalism. The Arab-Israeli struggle developed into a major ongoing conflict in a particularly sensitive region of the world and continues to the present day. The tipping point from nationalism to Islamism was the 1967 Arab-Israeli War. After that, the Palestinians became both radicalized and organized. What began as a battle for national existence and land took on a religious dimension that produced a continued breeding ground for both secular and religious terrorist groups. The former evolved into nationalist groups favoring a Palestinian state, the latter evolved into the Global Jihadists Movement, which sought the destruction of secular rule in other regional states.

The 1979 Iranian Revolution moved this development a step further, and left Ayatollah Khomeini's radical Islamic movement in control of a powerful regional state. The Iranians extended their diplomatic and religious propaganda presence to virtually all Islamic states within a decade, forcing both students and practitioners of diplomacy to study the impact of religion on diplomacy more carefully. For the first time, a major political movement committed to expanding international terror gained control of a significant national state entity. The political and diplomatic implications of this are outlined in the next chapter,

Both scholars and policy makers were slow to comprehend how fundamentally religious terrorism changes geostrategic considerations, both for good and ill. It undercut the existing intellectual paradigm that developed in the middle years of the twentieth century, when "modernization" brought about a secularization of society, which was supposed to reduce the influence of religion as a category of influence in public life.[5] Instead, modernization in some places created social crises that led directly to political radicalization of peoples, often using religions principles and organizations.

The religious dimension of terrorism spread out into other areas, and terrorism became a cottage industry across the region, with overtones of state and revolutionary strategy.[6] The growth of conflict in Afghanistan, plus conflict between Islamic Pakistan and Hindu India, reemphasized to many in the Islamic world the conflict between Islam and other faiths since the time of the Crusades. As Islamic societies became progressively less capable of dealing with the modern world, people's frustrations and hatreds transformed into Islamic radicalism, which expanded exponentially, as did the number of radical movements.[7]

Matters came to a head after the first Gulf war, when Islamic fundamentalists in Saudi Arabia were greatly disturbed by the presence of American troops there. These Islamicists drew on the veterans of the U.S.-sponsored efforts to build Islamic movements (including the Taliban, with Pakistani help) to overthrow the Russian puppet government in Afghanistan in the 1980s.[8] When the Russians left Afghanistan in 1989, the U.S. and its allies abruptly and very unwisely abandoned all interest in Afghanistan and its nascent Muslim movements. As a result, our current nemesis in Afghanistan, the Taliban, emerged victorious in a five-year struggle to govern Afghanistan by organizing an effective insurgency movement.

The Taliban sheltered Al Qaeda, which sought sanctuary with the Taliban, and both, working through other organizations including Iran, were behind a growing series of serious terror incidents against the U.S. in the 1990s: the 1993 attack on the New York World Trade Center, the 1996 bombing of the Kobar Towers complex in Saudi Arabia, the 1998 bombings of U.S. Embassies in Kenya and Dar es Salaam, and the 2000 attack on the USS *Cole*— the warm-ups, as it were, to the destruction of the World Trade Center on September 11, 2001.

Before 9/11, however, these other events were not "big enough on the radar" to attract much public concern. Terrorism officials in Washington had great difficulty getting the president and other key officials to focus on the emerging threat.[9] The destruction of the World Trade Center and concurrent attack on the Pentagon, however, got everyone's attention. An American intelligence officer, Michael Scheuer, writing under the pen name "Anonymous" in 2001, urged all Americans, not just his own intelligence colleagues, "to understand the historical and religious context in which bin Laden has acted and in which [the Taliban] emerged."[10]

Problems with awareness continued in the unfolding of America's counter-terrorist policy in the period from February/March 2002 to the present. In fact, one of the principal disconnects in the foreign policy/decision making process has been the growing gap between regional specialists in diplomacy, professors of religion, the military and the intelligence branches and technical and geostrategic thinkers on one hand, and senior policy makers and ideologues on the other. Common sense and collaboration in the initial phases of the post-9/11 terrorist response gave way to self-righteous insistence on policy in defiance of mounting evidence of failure.[11]

This was reflected almost immediately by inadequate policy and action. An initial focus on Afghanistan from September 2001 routed the Taliban and forced Al Qaeda into the battle of Tora Bora in early 2002. But the U.S. did not follow through with enough force or manpower. Unfortunately, bin Laden and his key leaders, including the Taliban, escaped into Pakistan, where they have since been unreachable. The neoconservative group clustered around Secretary Rumsfeld and Paul Wolfowitz in the defense department began to urge upon the government the strategy of democratizing the Middle East by first removing Saddam Hussein. They disregarded the views of the regional specialists in both the state and defense departments, as well as the vast majority of American experts in the region.[12]

The result has been as sad as it was predictable: The Iraqis were overjoyed to see Saddam gone, but they did not immediately and docilely flock to the American banner, as the Neoconservatives had insisted they would. With too few troops to lock the country down, security quickly became and remains a severe and increasing problem. Ethnic and religious forces began to jockey for power and build their own paramilitary forces. By early 2006, terrorist militias dominated the scene and disrupted political efforts of the U.S. and the Iraqi government to establish control, growing stronger steadily until the middle of 2007.

Al Qaeda and another group, al-Ansar, built up strong terrorist groups in Iraq. American sources estimate they had between three thousand and five thousand insurgents in Feb. 2004, and this grew to twenty thousand in the summer of 2005.[13] These groups disrupt Iraqi rebuilding efforts with sabotage, particularly in the oil industry, and prevent political reconciliation by attacks on citizens, and foreign civilian aid personnel.

The lesson is clear: diplomatic, assistance and intelligence efforts all have been severely hampered by underestimating the impact of American action or inaction in an environment which is poorly understood at the top. A principal reason, (certainly not the only one) was the lack of high-level understanding of the way terrorist groups built their philosophy of terrorism on religious belief to justify attacking other Islamic organizations as well as Christian and other groups. America had been there before—in South Vietnam of the 1960s, when the Buddhists built an opposition by the same means. The lessons of Vietnam were regarded as Cold War anachronisms, and our earlier hard-won national expertise in terrorist-insurgent warfare was ignored.[14]

In fact, *the* key truth in the present struggle is that the "War on Terrorism" is not a clash of civilizations—though many of its targets are in the West—the U.S., Spain, Britain—but a civil war within Islamic civilization between extremists who use violence to enforce their vision and a moderate majority who want such things as jobs, education, health care and dignity as they practice their faith. Neither we nor anyone else can "win" such a war on terrorism until we understand this basic situation and adapt to the fact that moderate Moslems are, and should be, our best allies.[15] Common sense and good political judgment both suggest we need to take more advantage of this situation.

IMPEDIMENTS

If such is the case, then our religious leaders as well as our politicians need to make a clear distinction between radical terrorists prone to violence and ordinary Muslims who do not share these views. There are two major impediments to doing this:

1. A distressing tendency in some quarters in American and Europe to consider all Muslims evil; and

2. Certain elements of the fifty-year history of American foreign policy in the Middle East.

The Rev. Pat Robertson and some other religious leaders here have proclaimed all Muslims "bad"—and these statements are well known in the Muslim world through Al-Jazeera (the Gulf TV station) and Al Qaeda's web pages. If ever there were a time for tolerance and informed understanding among Christians, it would seem to be now. It is slowly emerging, but has a long way to go.

American Muslim leaders were at first slow to realize the problem. Just after 9/11, a few even insisted that terrorism had nothing to do with Islam in the case of the World Trade Center attack. By 2004, however they were adjusting, worried that radicals would recruit American Muslims into terrorism. A fatwa (religious edict) against extremism and terrorism was issued in July 2005 by a group of North American Muslim scholars and has been signed by representatives of over two hundred fifty Islamic Centers. This follows Muslim efforts by Islamic authorities in Yemen to debate extremism with prisoners and other extremist supporters.[16]

Al Qaeda and the Taliban's basic strategy is to play up these attacks and slurs and provoke the U.S. to attack Muslims—whether in Afghanistan, Iraq or elsewhere—to showcase the brutality of the West. By reminding Muslims of prior humiliation under colonialism, they want to force changes toward extremist governments in Western-leaning Arab states and turn them into Iran-style Islamic "Republics," or worse.

By insisting that the Muslims hate us because of our freedoms, the Bush administration has played directly into this strategy and our military action in Iraq reinforces bin Laden's message. This has led to a steady and consistent growth in foreign terrorism in Iraq over the past three years. Iraq is now the Mecca for Islamic extremists, and the training ground for thousands of new recruits.[17]

The other impediment that makes this strategy possible is continuing American policies in the Middle East. The greater Islamic world is not so offended by our freedom, our personal and civil rights, and our separation of church and state, but as the leading American student of Al Qaeda, Milton Scheurman, notes, America is hated and attacked because Muslims believe they know precisely what the U.S. is doing in the Islamic World. They know partly because of Osama bin Laden's words, partly because of satellite television, but mostly because of the tangible reality of U.S. policies."[18]

What are these policies, in *their* eyes?

- U.S. support for Israel that appears woefully unbalanced to the Palestinians;

- U.S. occupation of Iraq and Afghanistan;

- U.S. and other Western troops on the Arabian Peninsula;

- U.S. support for corrupt, apostate and tyrannical Muslim governments;

- U.S. pressure on Arab energy producers to keep oil prices low; and

- U.S. support for Russia, China and India against their Muslim militants.

Clearly the problem is not simply more military action—that alone has not worked, has alienated our friends in the Middle East, and provided more grist for the extremist's mill. Theologians already know one of the biggest aspects of the problem. Rev. Susan Thistlehwaite, of the Chicago Theological seminary told a U.S. Institute of Peace meeting ". . . one area where work is greatly need in the United States is to promote more awareness of how the United States and its actions are viewed around the world."[19]—And this is from a theologian, not an international relations professor! We simply don't have a realistic sense of how they view us.

The Middle East is not the only area where the religion/politics mix creates life-threatening conflict and violence across the political landscape. Episodes of terrorism continue in Latin America, Central Asia, and even in Europe.

RELIGION'S IMPACT ON KEY GROUPS AND INDIVIDUALS'
WORLDVIEWS

In the Islamic case, the perception of political and social reverses over the past two centuries has promoted a feeling of humiliation and the desire to strike back. In other areas, such as the Balkans, religion is often tied to ethnic and national issues, a particularly destructive potion. The socioeconomic failure of regimes in the Middle East and elsewhere has created a sense of fear and anger that has contributed to this malaise. The young in Iran, Egypt, Algeria and many other places feel their situation is hopeless—no jobs and little prospect of betterment. They then turn to attacking their governments, most of which have good relations and ties to the U.S.

Osama bin Laden
Source: www.fbi.gov

In following this path, they are often led into Islamic radicalism. bin Laden, for example, has so shaped his view of Islam that he justifies war against women and children—specifically prohibited in the Koran. To argue with such individuals, one has to understand the roots of their beliefs (which really requires a good grounding in one's own faith), or one cannot penetrate others' selective use of scripture that is used to pervert the real meaning.[20] Thus religious doctrine becomes a direct political tool.

Somewhat different and less extreme in practice are the Hindu nationalist policies of the Bharatiya Janata Party (BPJ) in India.

Hinduism has the most flexible doctrine of the major religions, and the success of the BJP is due to its mixing Hindu doctrine/theology with political need to build support. The enables Hindus to resolve some larger issues, but it can also promote communalism in certain places—a tendency to see "us as exclusively correct," and the 'other' solely as an enemy."[21]

Similarly, the rise of Sinhalese Buddhist fundamentalism in Sri Lanka and the resultant Tamil guerrilla nationalist force, the Tamil Tigers, have mixed religion with politics to foment a bloody twenty-two-year civil war. The politico-religious mix on both sides of this fight has made peacekeeping exceptionally difficult—since there are no interests to blend and compromise, only ethno-religious doctrine buttressing implacable stances on both sides.[22]

INDIA

Courtesy of The Universtiy of Texas Libraries, The University of Texas at Austin

Religion underlies basic beliefs in other countries as well—the U.S., most of Western Europe, even China and Japan—but it is not normally toxically linked with politics in the same way it is in the Middle East and South Asia—at least for now.

A number of books have explained the development of terrorist worldviews and documented the creation of a *zeitgeist*, which is radically distant from Western conceptions of political philosophy, but has roots in various other appeals to martyrdom, identification of evildoers, etc.[23] R. Scott Appleby, a keen student of the sacred, underlines the issue succinctly:

> The Western myopia on this subject of religious power has been astounding. Christians of the United States, long accustomed to living in a religiously plural society governed by the principles of religious freedom, church-state separation, and the rule of law, seem to have forgotten the death-defying roots of their own tradition. Christians, like Muslims, have considered martyrdom a prime opportunity for holiness and, indeed, a direct ticket to heaven.[24]

Disturbingly, in the wake of 9/11, this is not only true abroad. Law officers in many American states are concerned that conservative militias, some with Christian ideologies, may be developing a tendency toward martyrdom. For example, a report on weapons of mass destruction vulnerabilities in Kentucky showed that the principal anxiety of the majority of the state's country sheriffs was focused on potential local militants, rather than foreign terrorists.[25]

At the highest levels, an improper understanding of religion and its impact on people can undercut strategic planning. Milton Scheurman, the author of *Through Our Enemies' Eyes* notes several points at which senior American leadership was unable to comprehend basic truths about bin Laden because it could not escape the classical modernist paradigm of the decreasing importance of religion.[26]

In our own intelligence community, retired CIA covert operative Robert Baer, speaking from the trenches, is even more critical of the need for agents at all levels who can get out and "start listening to people again, no matter how unpleasant the message is."[27] Religion cannot be studied by satellite—one needs to know how people think, especially those who don't start from the same place you do. This is the real objective of adequate cultural understanding, which is essential to any common sense approach to a complex issue.

This problem is not new in history, but it is particularly acute now with the rise of terrorism on a broader scale, and the growth of an ideological perspective in our own policy/decision makers who have great difficulty in getting beyond their own mindset. The media has been full of sobering examples of this combination over the past year: rigid neoconservative insistence that the Iraqi people would flock to the American standard of an invasion of Iraq;[28] major failures in weapons intelligence in Iraq;[29] and strong indications of intelligence "cooked" to support certain views.[30] Nor is it a partisan one—from controversy of the Tonkin Gulf incident through the misunderstanding of Buddhists during the Vietnam War, and on to the Carter Administration's handling of Iran, Democrats have been as fallible as Republicans.

Thus, when neither policy makers, diplomats, nor intelligence officers understood the impact of

Gulf of Tonkin Incident—USS Maddox fires upon three P-4 torpedo boats
Source: U.S. Navy Historical Center, Washington Navy Yard, Wikipedia, Painting by E.J. Fitzgerald

Khomeini's philosophy or the emotional content of this doctrine mixing faith and government, decisions went awry. One thoughtful scholar concludes, "Unfortunately, universal rationality is difficult to square with cultural-religious traditions."[31]

Those who have studied faith-based diplomacy note how easy it is for religious leaders to become enmeshed in politics:

> The range of cases make it clear that Christianity and Islam enjoy no monopoly on religious extremism. . . . The rate of killing accelerates, in fact, when the combatants on both sides claim religion as their motivation. The transcendent cause . . . is a source of renewal for warriors who otherwise might abandon a struggle that becomes protracted, exhausting and ambiguous in its political consequences."[32]

Moreover, faith can bring an additional leadership dynamic to politics:

> ". . . The religious leader is summoned to the political stage. The reduction of religion to ideology brings with it wrenching demands on the traditional religious figure. . . . Under pressure from the roiling forces of sectarian and ethnic conflict, driven by 'identity crises' that are fabricated or exaggerated for the purpose of drawing sharp battle lines, the monk (priest, rabbi, imam) becomes a spokesperson for and mobilizer of ordinary believers who can be convinced that the source of their poverty . . . lies not in corrupt and despotic regimes . . . but in the designs and plots of the ethnic or religious "others."[33]

This scenario has played itself out in the Middle East, South Asia and the Balkans; the same dynamic is afloat in Indonesia, the Philippines and potentially in Central Asia. It is especially true in those states which host American forces, which can too easily be made the target "other" by those who can generate enough emotional/religious backing.

This clearly poses potential strategic issues for our operations in Iraq, which are seen as a prelude to "bringing democracy to the region." It is also the reason why religious thinkers need to interact more regularly and intelligently with cultural and political specialists to test their understandings against one another. It wouldn't hurt if a few politicians joined in. This is common sense, bolstered by good judgment.

ORGANIZATIONAL ISSUES

The organizational impact of faith and faith issues has been recognized since the sixteenth century. The new spin today is the mix with religious doctrines that go against the modernization paradigm, and bring spiritual, or *so-called* "irrational," elements into active participation in the political, economic and military arenas. Ultimately, it is a question of values—which ones drive our societies and how do we integrate them with our other secular values?

The Russian Orthodox Church was subordinated to the State, after Stalin consolidated his power in the 1920s. The KGB therefore targeted religious groups, kept steady watch on them, and made sure that senior clerics were vetted and approved by the regime.[34]

Beginning in the 1980s and as a result of American support for the Islamic forces in Afghanistan, the KGB began to fear and target militant Islamic forces in the Soviet Union. This continues today, with special relevance to Chechnya and those Central Asian states where Islamic radicalism and terrorism has found a small foothold. This was exacerbated to some degree by negative blowback from the Soviet invasion of Afghanistan and the subsequent departure of Russian forces.

Perhaps the most effective use of religion as a counter-governmental political weapon in the Soviet Bloc was in Poland in the 1980s. There, the Catholic Church was able to help pry the communists out of power by working closely with the Polish Solidarity movement, with help from other countries including the U.S.[35]

Since the 1970s there have been a number of other instances where religious groups/churches have been involved in significant ways in politics. Most denominations in South Africa opposed South Africa across its over forty years of existence, and religious leaders were instrumental in minimizing violence as apartheid ended. In the rest of Africa, religious organizations have been extensively involved in relief efforts over the past fifty years. In the Philippines and East Germany, Catholics and Protestants respectively were instrumental in the revolutions of 1986 and 1989, resulting in changes of both governments.[36]

None of these events had the emotional impact of the two revolutions in the Middle East/Central Asia area. The Iranian Revolution of 1979 differed from these cases, as did the post-communist 1992 revolution in Afghanistan that brought the Taliban to power. In both these situations, a radical political movement based itself on the power of key religious leaders who became politicians. In Iran, the language of the mullahs became the dialog of politics, and the more secular Liberation movement could not fight both that and Khomeini's charisma.

Even the international language of the present Iranian regime is grounded in radical Shiite Islamic dialog—despite the fact that 70 percent of the people either ignore or actively reject it.[37] In 1979, it was almost impossible for the U.S. Embassy in Tehran to convince our colleagues in Washington that the rising Shia fundamentalism in Iran threatened the regime. All sections of the embassy had great difficulty making critical points to those who were not sensitized to what was happening.[38] Sadly, we have only marginally improved in the years since—and completely misfired in Iraq.

In Afghanistan, the Taliban was created by radical clerics with considerable help from the Pakistani Intelligence Service and substantial U.S. collaboration, plus aid. The Pakistani support continued until 9/11, and perhaps beyond; American support lapsed when the Soviets left Afghanistan. The Taliban drew on young people who had been trained in the dialog of the religious school—the maddrassehs. Fundamentalist clergy, who preach and teach a violent "war of civilization" view that would warm Samuel Huntington's (*Clash of Civilizations*) heart, run these schools.[39] The rapid withdrawal of the U.S. from the region after the defeat/ withdrawal of the Soviet Union in 1988 left a vacuum in Afghanistan, which was filled by several of these groups. In the civil war that followed, the Taliban emerged victorious—largely because no one else cared.[40]

The consequences of this development, coupled with the later American strategic decision *not* to continue major pursuit and corner the Al Qaeda forces after the Tora Bora battle, when key figures (including bin Laden) escaped, allowed the Taliban and its radical Muslim allies in Pakistan to reorganize. They began to reassert themselves in Afghanistan about the time U.S. Chief of Staff Gen. Richard Meyers

Tora Bora—A CH-47 helicopter drops off coalition force members into the Tora Bora region of Afghanistan in support of Operation Torii.
Soure: www.af.mil, Photo by Staff_Sgt. Jeremy T. Lock, USAF

prematurely declared an end to offensive operations there in November 2002. Pakistan remains the principal sanctuary of these groups, and the Pakistani government itself is infiltrated with Taliban sympathizers. This poses acute problems for both India and the U.S.

The sad result has been renewed and expanding guerrilla activity in Afghanistan and Pakistan, which has included seven attempts on Pakistani President Musharref's life. It has also enabled Al Qaeda to participate in the growing guerrilla war against U.S. forces in Iraq, which began to seriously interrupt the rebuilding of that country in the summer/fall of 2003. Allowing the Taliban and Al Qaeda to rebuild was one of the worst long-term strategic blunders the Bush administration made (Rumsfeld was the principal culprit).

The principal problem with Al Qaeda is that the U.S. has had far too little real knowledge of its organization, and have improved that only marginally since 9/11.[41]   One intelligence officer described the loose organization as "franchising terrorism; bin Laden is the Ray Kroc [McDonald's] of Terrorism." Our present level of understanding amounts to hearsay.[42]

Downplaying this organized religious zeal was doubly unfortunate, because it opened up the unnerving prospect of a radical Islamic takeover of Pakistan by forces that would almost certainly break ties with the U.S., and then reinsert Muslim guerrillas into Kashmir to provoke a confrontation with an India that remains at partial mobilization despite recent peace overtures. This could far too easily lead to a confrontation in which one or both countries' nuclear arsenals could be brought into play.[43]

While the India-Pakistan border shows the most serious current consequence of mis-estimating the organizational impact of fundamentalism gone bad, it is not the only place where religious forces ideologically hostile to the West are creating problems— Algeria, Egypt, Sudan and Iraq come quickly to mind.

Iraq is where the most immediate danger lies, as the U.S. has tried to get the country organized well enough to turn over control to a local government. The simple U.S. goal of establishing a democratic government has proved impossible given the fervent Shia support for democracy that would leave the largest of Iraq's three principal groupings with a dominant role, with Sunnis and Kurds rejecting this outcome. The assumption that Iraq could be made democratic in four months was either incredibly naïve or delusional, given both the guerrilla war and the tripartite ethnic division of the country into Kurdish, Sunni and Shiite tribal views on what democracy means. Neither American thinking nor perseverance has reached the requisite levels for dealing successfully with this situation.

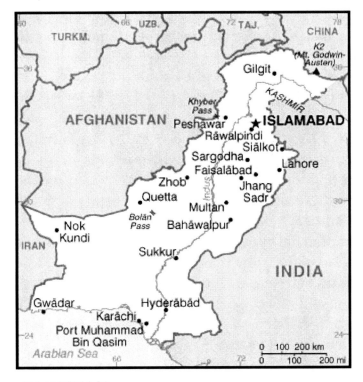

PAKISTAN

Courtesy of The Universtiy of Texas Libraries, The University of Texas at Austin

Special problems of Religion and Terrorism

In addition to learning more about religion and its impact, we also need to abandon the conventional idea that religion necessarily diminishes in importance as societies develop. Instead, accept and use the truth that development sometimes brings social crises (as it has done in the Middle East and elsewhere) which themselves will raise political and social problems in religious guises. In these cases, absent countervailing pressures, people seek a version of religion that increases their hostility while at the same time giving them emotional and political support against challenges they feel increasingly incapable of meeting.

Until Westerners, from agents and analysts including White House and departmental staffers, to cabinet members and presidents, have a sense of how Islamic, Hindu, and Buddhist fundamentalists think, they cannot properly match their strategies with their actions.

A good place to begin is with the idea of Holy War. The West does not comprehend the "contemporary phenomenon of Holy War which has become an object of suspicion from both the secular and the Christian perspectives."[44] The Islamic concept of *Jihad* has been severely warped away from its true meaning by those who promote violent extremism. Once one begins to understand Islamic doctrine, one quickly learns that the real conflict created by the Islamic radicals is between themselves and the vast majority of Muslims who do not and cannot accept a badly distorted theology. It may be humbling for proud American politicians, statesmen and intelligence folk to turn to theology for important political clues, but it is vital, as intelligence scholar John Keegan says, "to find a way into the fundamentalist's mindset and to overcome it from within."[45]

Along with better understanding, there must come a better education of a generation of diplomats, politicians and religious authorities, as well as an increase in general public awareness.

Most scholars and analysts know that it makes no difference how smart you are if you can't communicate successfully with those above you in the hierarchical chain—or the public. This requires that those at the top understand the parameters of what is being presented and discussed. America is not now ready for the next twenty years.

Donald H. Rumsfeld, former Secretary of Defense, and Afghanistan President Hamid Karzai at the Presidential Palace, Kabul, Afghanistan on April 13, 2005.
Source: U.S. Dept of State

Lest one believe that this is a trivial or an academic exercise, understand that if politicians and other senior figures do not understand the consequences of wrong-headedness, they will be taught the consequences the hard way. Secretary of Defense Rumsfeld and the president, as well as a number of senators and representatives, were instructed by events on the ground and the 2006 congressional elections and subsequently, which cost their party control of Congress and left the president's popularity below 30 percent heading into the 2008 campaign.

Although U.S. leaders initially rightly decided to confront bin Laden with military means, their recognition of the motivation and destructive power of the bin Laden phenomenon remains superficial.[46] It is not clear whether American perseverance will remain strong enough to get us through the learning process to be able to cope with the deeper issues bin Laden and his ilk raise.

Part of the issue here is hubris and arrogance, much of which has been reflected in the debate of the past few years as to whether America is an "empire" or merely has primacy, and what that means.[47] There has been much criticism of the "War on Terror" and its implications in terms of Patriot Acts, military activity and diplomacy. What are the "right" goals for the U.S.? Are we strong enough militarily? How hard should we pursue them and at what cost to other domestic policies? Is the issue as simple as it is posed by Bernard Lewis: "The range of American policy options in the [Middle East] region is reduced to two alternatives, both disagreeable: Get tough or get out," or is it more subtle and nuanced?

If we are to deal successfully with the world of the next few years, we—you, me, and others around us—have to get to know the territory. That means increasing general knowledge and learning from experts who are familiar with the cultures, and knowing the theological-political arguments of groups, and even nations. This is the key to good judgment on public issues. When Willie Sutton was asked why he robbed banks, he replied, "Because that's where the money is." For understanding, we have to go where the knowledge is. For terrorism, that means looking at the problem of nuclear and biological terror—advanced weapons, stolen, developed or purchased, in the hands of terrorists.[48] Thus far, except for one episode in Japan and several post-9/11 letters in the U.S., there has been no major use of these weapons yet. However, U.S. intelligence sources believe this is one of Al Qaeda's principal aims for the future.[49]

If one wants to understand the world of the terrorist, one has to find a way in. This poses ethical and moral dilemmas, particularly for the intelligence and media communities, but these will have to be dealt with in one way or another. In sum, the gap between those that know terrorism and religion and those that know intelligence, diplomacy and defense needs to be considerably lessened.

How to Proceed?

On the political side, a refined understanding of how religion interacts with politics is key to producing a policy approach to the problem that pulls religious moderates and natural allies along with us. The disastrous international slide in U.S. popularity over the past two years is especially ironic for a country that has promoted religious freedom. For example, in mid-2001, before the 9/11 boost, virtually all countries except North Korea showed well above 50 percent approval of America. In February 2005, the widely respected PIPA program showed only three of twenty-two countries surveyed showing over 50 percent, the highest of which was Iran, believe it or not with a 69 percent favorable rating.[50] A vast majority of Iran's citizens like us because they greatly dislike their government. In traditional Middle Eastern terms, "the enemy of my enemy is my friend."

The "either with us or against us" American politics of the post-9/11 period have and still are creating the clash of civilizations that Huntington warns about. Without a different tack, stressing the basic harmony between religions on key points (more true to our own values), we will find far fewer allies against the true terrorists than we need in those parts of the world which do not share our own faith. This is simply good judgment, even common sense.

This is but one indication of how hard it is to make the simple case for a better understanding of our adversaries when it involves taking new paths and thinking new thoughts. Such a deeper understanding of some critical issues still seems pressing five years and counting after 9/11.

---

[1] Hoffman, Bruce. *Inside Terrorism.* (New York: Columbia Univ. Press, 2006), pp. 2-41; see also Dekmejian, R. H. *Spectrum of Terror* (Washington: CQ Press, 2007), pp. 15-21.

[2] Dekmejian, *op. cit.*, pp. 35-6.

[3] Joes, Anthony. *America and Guerilla Warfare.* (Lexington: University of Kentucky Press, 2004), chs. 9 and 10.

[4] Hoffman, *op. cit.*, pp. 53-80; Dekmejian, *op. cit.*, ch. 6.

[5] Rubin, Barry. "Religion and International Affairs," ch. 3 in *Religion, The Missing Dimension of Statecraft*, Douglas Johnson and Cynthia Sampson, (eds.) (New York: Oxford Univ. Press, 1994).

[6] Hunter, F. Robert. *The Palestinian Uprising*. University of California Press, 1991; Barry Rubin (ed.) *The Politics of Terrorism*. chs. 2, 3 and 7. (Johns Hopkins Foreign Policy Institute, 1989).

[7] Lewis, Bernard. powerfully recounts this process in his two books *What Went Wrong? Western Impact and Middle Eastern Response*. (Oxford: Oxford Univ. Press, 2002); and *The Crisis of Islam: Holy War and Holy Terror. (*New York: The Modern Library, 2003).

[8] Rashid, Ahmad. *Taliban: Militant Islam, Oil, and Fundamentalism in Central Asia*. (New Haven: Yale Univ. Press, 2000), chs. 1, 6 and 14.

[9] Tenet, George. *At the Center of the Storm*. (New York: HarperCollins, 2007), chs. 7 and 8.
[10] Anonymous. *Through Our Enemies' Eyes*. (Washington: Brasey's, 2002), p. xii and ch. 1.

[11] Risen, James. *State of War*. (New York: Free Press, 2006), ch. 7.

[12] A good overall review of this subject can be found in an excellent series of articles in the January 2004 Atlantic Monthly. The academic case is cogently set out in Mearsheimer, John and Stephen Walt. "Iraq: An Unnecessary War," *Foreign Policy*, January/February 2003, pp. 50-59; and the gap between regionalists and geostrategists amply illustrated in Hentz, James (ed.). *The Obligations of Empire: The United States' Grand Strategy at Century's Dawn: The Globalist/Regionalist Debate*. (Lexington: Univ Press of Kentucky, 2004). A leading regional scholar's point of view can be found in the Foreign Policy Institute's *WIRE*, vol. 12, no. 1, January 2004: Pollack, Kenneth M. "America and the Middle East after Saddam." For the intelligence side, see Tenet, *op. cit.*, ch. 11.

[13] Rashid, op. cit., Ch. 1.

[14] Our long struggle with insurgency in South Asia is well documented (Joes, *American and Guerilla Warfare, op. cit.*, ch. 7 and pp. 323-32); but its potential application to the Middle East is only just now being discovered. See also Khalidi, Rashid. *Resurrecting Empire; Western Footprints and America's Perilous Path in the Middle East* (Boston: Beacon Press, 2005), pp. v-xvi and pp. 128-30.

[15] The clearest explanation of why this is so may be found in Aslan, Reza. *No god but God* (New York: Random House, 2006), chs. 9 and 10.

[16] "Muslim Leaders Confront Terror Threat Within Islam," by Laurie Goodstein, Sept. 2, 2005, *The New York Times*; "Koranic Duels Ease Terror," by James Brandon, *The Christian Science Monitor*, p. 1.

[17] *Defeating the Jihadists*, A Century Foundation Task Force Report, The Century Foundation, 2005; and Danner, Mark. "Taking Stock of the Forever War, *The New York Times Magazine*, September 11, 2005, pp. 46-86.

[18] "CIA Insider: The Threat We Refuse to Get," *The Washington Post*, July 11, 2004, p. B01. More comprehensive, by the same author, is Anonymous. *Imperial Hubris*, (New York: Brasey's Inc., 2004).

[19] *Building Interreligious Trust in a Climate of Fear*. U.S. Institute of Peace Special Report 99, February 2003, p. 9.

[20] Anonymous. *Through Our Enemies' Eyes. op. cit.* chs. 1 and 2 focus on bin Laden. The direct link to terrorism is well traced in Hoffman's *Inside Terrorism*. op. cit., ch. 4. A complete rundown on bin Laden can be found in Randal, Jonathan. *Osama: The Making of a terrorist*. (New York: Alfred A. Knopf, 2004).

[21] Johnstone, Douglas. *Faith-Based Diplomacy: Trumping Realpolitik*. (ed.), (Oxford Univ. Press, 2003), ch. 3. For a more penetrating discussion of the whole region, see Bjorkman, James. *Fundamentalism, Revivalists and Violence in South Asia*. (San Francisco: Riverdale Co., 1988).

[22] Johnstone, *Faith-Based Diplomacy, op cit.*, ch. 4; and Bjorkman, *Fundamentalism...* op. cit., ch. 7.

[23] Rashid, Ahmed. *Taliban, op. cit.*, especially chapters 1-3, 6 and 8; and Cooley, John K. *Unholy Wars: Afghanistan, America and International Terrorism*. (Pluto Press, 2002), documents the growth of radical views among the dispossessed.

[24] Johnstone, *Faith-based Diplomacy...* op. cit., p. 231.

[25] Source is a member of the team that interviewed officials in all of Kentucky's 120 counties; the study itself is held very closely.

[26] Anonymous. *Through Our Enemies Eyes*, op. cit., Introduction, chs. 1, 4, 14 and 15.

[27] Baer, Robert. *See No Evil*. (New York: Crown Publishers, 2002, pp. 67, 81; quote from p. 271.

[28] Fallows, James. "Blind into Baghdad," *The Atlantic*, vol. 293, No. 1, January-February 2004, pp. 52-77.

[29] Pollack, Kenneth M. "Spies, Lies, and Weapons: What Went Wrong," *The Atlantic*, vol. 293, no. 1, January-February 2004, pp. 78-92; Tenet, op. cit., pp. 331-8, and ch. 24.

[30] Hersh, Seymour M. "The Stovepipe: How Conflicts between the Bush Administration and the intelligence community marred the reporting on Iraq's weapons," *The New Yorker*, October 27, 2003, pp. 7-87. Tenet, op. cit., pp. 341-51.

[31] Seliktar, Ofira. *Failing the Crystal Ball Test: The Carter Administration and the Fundamentalist Revolution in Iran*. (New York: Praeger, 2000), chs. 1, 2 and 6.

[32] Johnstone, *Faith-Based Diplomacy, op. cit.,* p. 233.

[33] Ibid, p. 234.

[34] Andrews, Christopher and Vasili Mitrokhin. *The Sword and the Shield: The Mitrokhin Archive and the Secret History of the KGB.* (New York: Basic Books, 1999), especially ch. 29.

[35] Ibid, Ch. 29.

[36] Descriptions of these activities can be found in *Religion, the Missing Dimension...,* op. cit.; and Crocker, Chester et. al. (eds.) *Herding Cats.* (Washington: U.S. Institute of Peace, 1999), chs. 7 and 11.

[37] See *The Economist,* January 27, 2004, pp. 12-13 and 19-21; as well as Stemple, John D. *Inside the Iranian Revolution* (Bloomington, IN: Indiana University Press, 1981), especially chs. 5 and 13.

[38] Stempel. *Inside the Iranian Revolution,* op. cit., ch. 14.

[39] Huntington, Samuel P. *The Clash of Civilizations and the Remaking of World Order.* (New York: Simon and Schuster, 1996), especially pp. 109-19 and 174-82.

[40] Cooley. *Unholy Wars.* op. cit., ch. 8.

[41] Tenet. op. cit. pp. 422-5.

[42] Anonymous. *Through our Enemies' Eyes.* op. cit., The entire book outlines bin Laden's life, character, motivation and tactics, chs. 1-5 constitute the short course.

[43] See, for example, *The Washington Post National Weekly Edition,* January 12-18, 2007, p. 17.

[44] Quoted from Johnson, James Turner. *The Holy War Idea in Western and Islamic Thought.* (State College: Penn State Univ. Press, 1997) p. 19; and *Through our Enemies' Eyes.* op. cit., p. 4.

[45] Keegan, John. *Intelligence in War.* (New York: Alfred Knopf, 2003), p. 319.

[46] Anonymous. *Through Our Enemies' Eyes.* op. cit., p. 3.

[47] Two excellent contrasting views of this can be found in Bacevich, Andrew J. *American Empire: The Realities and Consequences of U.S. Diplomacy.* (Boston: Harvard University Press, 2002); and Todd, Emmanuel. *After the Empire: The Breakdown of the American Order.* (New York: Columbia University Press, 2003). Perhaps the best and most balanced offering on this subject is Odom, William E. and Robert Dujarric. *America's Inadvertent Empire.* (New Haven: Yale Univ. Press, 2004).

[48] For a well-rounded approach to both topics, see Ferguson, Charles and William C. Potter. *The Four Faces of Nuclear Terrorism.* (Monterey, CA: Monterey Institute of International Studies, 2004), chs. 1 and 7; and Guillemin, Jeanne. *Biological Weapons: From the Invention of state sponsored programs to contemporary bioterrorism.* (New York: Columbia Univ. Press, 2005), Introduction and ch. 10.

[49] Tenet. op. cit., p. 279.

[50] http://www.forbes.com/2007/08/22/bush-anti-americanism-cx_0823oxfordanalytica_print.html, September 14, 2007.

CHAPTER 6
IRAN & AMERICA

It is better to know some of the questions than all of the answers.

—James Thurber

FOR ABOUT TWENTY-SIX YEARS BETWEEN 1953 AND 1979, American relations with Iran were close and advantageous to both sides. For the past twenty-eight years, relations between Iran and America have been about as bad as they could be, following the revolution that deposed the Shah in February 1979 and fundamentally reorganized Iranian society.

Only older Americans remember the subsequent hostage crisis and constant attacks on the U.S., but all of us have heard Iranian leaders continue to call the U.S. "The Great Satan." They consider us the bane of the planet, and challenge our policies throughout the Middle East and the world. If Iran were a less centrally located power in a vital region, and if it was not our principal antagonist in terms of our involvement in Iraq and Arab-Israeli peace efforts, we could simply dismiss or ignore its radical Islamic leadership, but we cannot. Therefore, common sense tells us we especially need to understand *this* adversary if we are to develop sound judgment in dealing with it. After all, we maintained diplomatic relationships with Germany in the 1930s and Russia during the Cold War, even if the invective flew.

Iran's theocratic government is unique and difficult to understand in traditional terms. The country is ruled by a supreme ayatollah, Ali Khamenei, in an autocratic and dictatorial manner. Elections are held for many government positions from city council to the president, but the lists of candidates are controlled by the theocracy, especially the Guardians Council, which reports directly to Supreme Ayatollah Khamenei and is controlled by him. The Council, with both clerical and secular members, is the dominant force in government and can even annul actions of Parliament.

The prime question is *how* do we deal with such a country? Iran is far too important to ignore, too big to bully, and capable of either significantly helping or hindering our efforts in the entire Middle East. At the end of his excellent historical study, *The Persian Puzzle*, former National Security Council official Kenneth Pollack summed up contemporary U.S. relations with Iran as follows:

> We must sort through the myriad pieces of our own relationship with this troubled and troubling nation, while also sorting out our equally difficult relations with the rest of the world.[1]

Ray Takeyh, another leading expert, concludes much the same thing:

> The best manner of dealing with such a state is through employment of the full range of diplomatic, political, and economic tools. The U.S. would be wise to abandon the rhetoric of the early Reagan years and the policies of the Cold War era. In the end, America's determination to stabilize the Middle East requires a more imaginative approach for the Islamic Republic of Iran.[2]

Unfortunately, a generation of hostility has taken its toll, been reciprocated on both sides, and been further emphasized in the current period of American unilateralism. As the Iraq war has wound down, voices from the neoconservative side of the administration say "Iran is next," or "Iran is the member of the axis of evil which can do the most damage to us." Many see these comments as the warm-up to a major military move against Iran. Those who make these statements hinting at war with Iran do so with little regard for the reality of the dynamics of the situation and the power of Iran, or with the complexities of American relations involving Iran and Iraq. They also slight our regional involvement in the Arab-Israeli dispute and attendant regional issues with Lebanon and Syria, all of which involve Iran.

IRAN

Courtesy of The Universtiy of Texas Libraries, The University of Texas at Austin

The question of how we deal with Iran, including Iran's capacity to deal with us, is often asked without reference to Iran itself—its post-revolutionary politics, economic conditions or military capabilities. It is vital that the U.S. approach Iranian issues without succumbing to the anger, ideology, and mythology of the past. The stakes are too great for a petulant, uninformed, chest-thumping policy. There are enough historical issues already on the table including money owed to each country by the other, the status of American diplomatic property, and weapons purchases.

Given the U.S. track record in Iraq as well as Iran, it is vital that the U.S. government should undertake a thorough, sober, realistic review of Iran's politics, culture, and military possibilities for mischief before acting precipitously. At that point, the U.S. can look with more confidence at the realistic options available and carefully assess which ones make the most sense in terms of our own capabilities and limitations. As personal development guru Stephen Covey advises, "If your ladder is leaning against the wrong wall, climbing higher and faster will not get you where you want to go."

IRAN'S ROAD SINCE 1979

Those forty-five and older remember the Shah's Iran—loyal U.S. ally against Communism and a modernizing monarchy seeking to make Iran a regional, if not a world, power in oil and energy. Iran remains a principal source of oil and gas—and America continues to have serious concerns about access on reasonable terms to the region's energy resources. The subsequent trauma of the Iranian Revolution and the hostage crisis, as well as the twenty-eight years of hostility between our two countries, has shaped a culture of confrontation that hinders important diplomatic and political work for both countries.

The overthrow of the Shah in February 1979 and the rise of Ayatollah Ruholla Khomeini to power flipped Iran from loyal ally to revolutionary regime based on a religious ideology focused on hatred of all things Western, and especially of the U.S.—the "Great Satan." Gone in the changeover was the Israeli Trade Mission in Tehran; in came the first Palestinian Embassy. In the course of a year, Khomeini and his Islamic radical faction shunted aside their rivals and established the first theocratic government in Iran in several hundred years (and the only one on the planet today which prefers salvation to economic development). Khomeini, as the *veliyat-e-fagih* (supreme leader) ruled without challenge.[3] His successor, Khamenei has the same power, but not the emotional dominance.

Abroad, Iran faced an eight-year war with Iraq, which forced it to settle the U.S. hostage crisis and return our embassy officers and staff.[4] From 1980-88, Iran and Iraq lost over three-quarters of a million people: including one hundred thousand Iranian children between the ages of nine and thirteen—the Basij, who were used to clear mine fields while seeking martyrdom for Allah. Iranian armed forces slowly grew stronger, and have remained combat-ready ever since.

At home, Iran floundered, unemployment rose to 70-80 percent in the 1980s before stabilizing around 25-30 percent in the late 1990s. Currency collapsed, with the value of the dollar rising from seventy rials to four thousand rials. Middle class Iran was squeezed. By the mid-1980s, over three million Iranians had emigrated. In 1979, Iran's population was thirty-four million; now it is seventy-two million. Over half of the population is under 30 years old, a result of a post-revolution baby boom.

The politics of Iran evolved in a direction very unfamiliar to Western thought, and the governmental structure was almost as hard for Iranians to understand as for foreigners. Iranians had to support the Revolution to participate in politics, but as the government evolved, three different factions emerged.

The first group, radical clerics and their allies, led by Supreme Leader Khomeini and after his death, his successor, Khamenei, were hard-line radical conservatives who believed in control of the government by the theocracy. They took over and still control the key institutions—the military, the intelligence services and the foreign ministry, plus the Guardians Council. Their economic policies are based on state control of key sectors of the economy (under trusted clerics, of course). This radical faction also took over and created foundations—"bonyads"—ostensibly to protect the peoples' money—but in reality to also serve as factional slush funds. They dismiss democratic pluralism, and insist upon control over the society.

The second group, the pragmatists, was led by Hojatollah Hashemi Rafsanjani, one of the few original revolutionary leaders who escaped death in June 1981, when persons unknown blew up Iranian Republican Party headquarters. He was president from 1989-1997, and he and his supporters in the commercial sector (the "Bazaarees") and elsewhere favored more cultural freedom, and private rather than state control of the economy. They believe Iran's future depends upon integrating itself into the world economy, joining in globalization. Their emphasis on cultural and economic freedom began to alter "the nature of the relationship between state and society. The declared mission of the government was no longer provision of salvation but delivering on its practical pledges."[5]

That set the stage for the 1997 presidential elections, where the third group, led by a more liberal cleric upset the hard-line conservative candidate for president with 70 percent of the vote. President Mohammad Khatami and more liberal advisors took over the executive branch and the Parliament—Majles. This became a time of liberalization—some rigorous Islamic cultural restrictions were removed, and efforts were made to open up the economy. This provoked a strong negative reaction by hard-line radicals that led to riots in 1999 and 2002.[6] Faced with a real crisis, Khatami refused to lead an open revolt against the hard-liners, and though he won reelection in 2002, his inability to make progress in democratizing the system eventually eroded his support. He tried to get a law through the Guardians Council that would prevent them from banning legislation, but the radical hard-liners held fast.

This attack on their privileges energized the radical hard-liners, who subsequently gained a parliamentary majority in the February 2005 elections. In June 2005 Iran elected a new president—a hard-line radical fundamentalist, Mahmoud Ahmadinejad, who promised better economic times. However, as time has passed, he also called for the destruction of Israel, invited Europe to make a place for Jewish refugees, and denied the Holocaust.[7]

The unremitting hostility toward the West and especially the U.S. by the hard-liners hindered both Rafsanjani's and Khatami's efforts to improve relations. The *Catch-22* of Iranian politics is that the economic goals of the pragmatists and the reformers cannot be met while the regime spews hostility toward other countries. This is a problem for both Iran and the U.S., but a bigger one for President Ahmadinejad, who campaigned on an economic betterment pledge. Unless he can deliver substantially more than he has done so far, his chances of retaining office in the 2009 elections are not good.

IRANIAN MILITARY CAPABILITIES AND FOREIGN POLICY

While there are several conflicting strands to Iran's foreign policy, all have been dominated by radical clerics. The bias has been anti-American and anti-Western. Iranian Foreign Ministry, intelligence and "Ministry of National Guidance" (cultural propaganda) personnel have spread far and wide, espousing Islamic fundamentalism in the Middle East and reaching as far as Burma, Malaysia and Indonesia.

In the beginning, this foreign outreach was part of the Iranian revolutionaries' classical export-the-revolution view. Shunned by the world diplomatic community after taking U.S. diplomats hostage in November 1979, and stunned by the failure of the world to support them against the Iraqi attack in 1980, the Iranians redoubled efforts to explain their actions. Their goal was to build like-minded revolutionary groups and to persuade these groups, and other countries, to push Iran's views and support them. From these roots grew close Iranian links with Hezbollah in Lebanon and Hamas and the Popular Front for the Liberation of Palestine (PFLP) in the West Bank, which was controlled by Israel. Since many of the original Iranian Islamic revolutionaries got their training from these groups, there is a strong intermix of trained professional revolutionaries on both sides. Each group increases the paranoia of the other.

Militarily, Iran fought the bloody eight-year war with Iraq, 1980-88, and emerged with a combat-hardened military. It currently has a combat capability substantially better than, and four times as big as, the Iraqi forces the U.S. defeated in 2003. While much of Iran's equipment is out of date and poorly maintained by U.S. standards, it has far better internal cohesion and far better morale that the Iraq forces, plus a highly developed insurgency capability (some of which is now on display in Iraq).[8] In sum, it would do serious damage to any attacking force, and could sustain a considerable insurgency, especially in Iranian cities. Given the present state of U.S. military involvement elsewhere, major engagement on this front is very dangerous to even consider.

The Pasdaran (Revolutionary Guards IRG) with one hundred thousand army and twenty thousand naval personnel, also control Iran's SHEHAB 3 medium range missiles. Additional potential guerilla forces, the Basij (ninety thousand active and three hundred thousand reserve) give the regime an enhanced homeland capability for defense and guerilla warfare as well. The Iranian Quds (Jerusalem) Brigade has substantial capability to wage guerilla and insurgent warfare, and connections with such forces in other countries, including Iraq, Syria and Lebanon.

They have been well trained, with substantial links to Hamas, the PFLP and others less well known, and it is these groups or their surrogates who have aided and supported terrorist activities against the West, and in Lebanon in 2006.

Other Iranian forces include the regular Navy. It has limited capacity, mostly missile patrol boats, manned by eighteen thousand sailors. However, in combination with the IRG navy forces, Iran can mount a solid mine warfare effort, as it tried to do in 1987-88 against tanker passage in the Persian Gulf. The Air Force is the weakest of the Iranian services, with only fifteen thousand men and three hundred combat aircraft, many not operational, in nine fighter-attack squadrons. It has a modest airlift capability of three B-707s and one B-747.

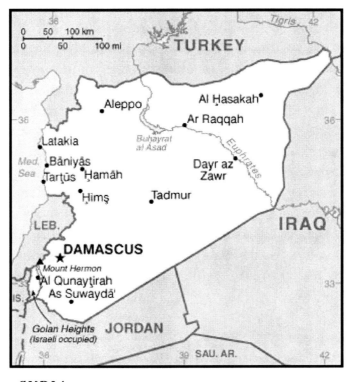

SYRIA

Iran's basic foreign policy dilemma is that it needs greater contact with the West to develop economically, but the reigning Islamic conservative hard-liners do not want even minimal relations with the U.S. During the Khatami period, the radical hard-liners mounted major efforts to block Iran's overtures to the U.S., and since the return of the radical conservatives to power in 2005, Iran has toyed with Western protests over its processing of uranium while continuing to develop its nuclear capability. It also seeks non-Western economic partners such as China and other Asian states to provide the goods it needs. Iran's recent $30 billion, ten-year oil deal with China gives it more leverage than it has had in a decade.

Militarily, the Iranian government fears what the U.S. could do to it, but understands, on some level, that Iran cannot achieve its goals without some kind of accommodation.

Thus official Iran moves between minimal cooperation with, and hate of, the U.S. The paradox is that opinion surveys in Iran routinely show that around 55 percent of Iranians *like* America. Coping with this kind of complex political situation calls for the best and most sophisticated understanding and analysis of which our country is capable. The danger that Iran's military and insurgency capabilities present for our forces in Iraq and for our aims elsewhere in the Middle East requires deft and careful handling if we are not to put ourselves in serious harm's way. Ideology that dismisses sound analysis, such as that applied to Iraq, is a serious danger and extremely harmful. Common sense as well as deep insight is required to a very high degree on this and related issues.

U.S. RELATIONS WITH IRAN

Hostility and distrust have pervaded contemporary U.S.-Iran relations since the revolution. Since 1979 the U.S. has had to deal with a leadership cadre whose major pillar of support is hatred of the U.S., even though there is much popular appreciation of the U.S.

In the background have been a series of international terrorist incidents that the U.S. believes Iranians were behind, or supported through their Hezbollah proxies. These incidents range from the 1983 bombings of the U.S. Embassy and the U.S. Marine barracks in Lebanon, which killed 242 U.S. Marines; the 1996 Khobar Towers bombing in Saudi Arabia which killed 19 and destroyed U.S. military housing; the 1998 destruction of our embassies in Nairobi and Dar es Salaam; and the bombing of the USS *Cole* in 2000 at the dock in Yemen.[9]

Nineteen Airmen died and hundreds were injured in the terrorist attack at Khobar Towers in Dhahran, Saudi Arabia, on June 25, 1996.
Source: www.af.mil

In recent years, the U.S. has settled on three major goals; it wants Iran:

1. To stop seeking the wherewithal to develop nuclear weapons;

2. To stop supporting terrorism; and

3. To cease interfering in the Middle East Peace process between Arabs and Jews.

The USS Cole after a suicide bombing attack against the U.S. Navy on October 12, 2000, in the Yemeni port of Aden
Source: Wikipedia, U.S. Navy photo

The nuclear issue is currently paramount, and involves a significant time element. The Iranians are preparing to make weapons-grade uranium, yet they deny their intent to make nuclear weapons. Distrust of their motives is widespread, with America leading the list. The Europeans negotiated a temporary halt to Iranian uranium enrichment activities in 2005, and after some fluffing around, U.S. Secretary of State Condoleezza Rice lined the U.S. up behind the Europeans' efforts to get a permanent cessation of enrichment to weapons grade levels.

After much maneuvering, the UN voted sanctions in December 2006. Iran regards Western and U.S. offers as humiliating, fears the U.S. really wants to overthrow the regime, and says it will not accept an agreement to freeze nuclear activities. Major oil deals with China and trade deals with Russia leave Iran in a position of strength.[10]

Time is narrowing—most say two to five years—to get an agreement before Iran has reached the point where it can join the nuclear club on its own, as Pakistan and India have done.

With respect to the issue of support for terrorism, matters got worse in the summer of 2006, when Hezbollah forces in Lebanon, aiding their Palestinian allies, began to rain missiles (provided by Iran) onto Israeli territory. This provoked an Israeli invasion of Lebanon that inflicted massive damage on Lebanon's infrastructure, especially in Shiite areas. Both sides eventually pulled back, but the internal struggle in Lebanon goes on.

Iran supports its Shia brethren in Iraq, but it has been cautious. During the U.S. invasion of Iraq, there was some businesslike, positive U.S.-Iran communication, but that gradually tapered off, which has been unfortunate. Even the hard-line clerics have been willing to talk in crisis situations, as they did during the U.S. invasion of Afghanistan in 2001, and at the beginning of the U.S. invasion of Iraq.

Iran under President Ahmadinejad has kept Iranian ties with anti-Israeli groups in place, and weapons shipments to Palestinian radicals and fundamentalists continue. Continued and substantial support for Palestinian terrorists, coupled with a hard-line stance on any potential peace and hostility to the Palestinian President offer little short-term hope.

To Talk or to Fight?

The ongoing debate on Iran has been whether to confront Iran with force or to seek an accommodation. In the 1990s, serious U.S. efforts to seek broader agreement with Iran had largely come to nothing because of Iranian intransigence. Even when that eased, American domestic politics prevented progress. American conservatives prevented President Bill Clinton from agreeing to a major deal involving Amoco and the National Iranian Oil Company in 1995, a deal that the clerical regime had already approved. That would have placed American businessmen in key positions in the Iranian oil industry. Iranian radicals frustrated several of President Khatami's moves that threatened to make concrete progress, even a positive response to the 1999 easing of sanctions on a few Iranian consumer exports—pistachios and carpets—and shipping of U.S. food and medicine was blocked.

A watershed of sorts occurred after the destruction of the World Trade Center on 9/11. At first, Iran was very cooperative toward our invasion of Afghanistan—even helping to put together the government of President Hamid Karzai, which still rules. In fact, the Iranians dislike the Sunni-dominated Taliban intensely for their earlier 1998 killing of nine Iranian diplomats assigned to the Afghan city of Herat. Some elements of the Iranian security forces gave sanctuary to some Al Qaeda forces initially, while Khatami's government rounded up others and kept them in custody. This

Hamid Karzai, President of Afghanistan
Source: DOD photo by R. D. Ward, www.defenselink.mil

would be an issue on which there is probably substantial room for maneuver, since Iran generally dislikes Al Qaeda, though it is not above cooperating with Iranian-supported groups like Hezbollah.

Even limited cooperation faded after President Bush's "Axis of Evil" remarks during his 2002 State-of-the Union speech, when he named Iran part of the axis and greatly increased Iranian fears of an assault by the U.S. Fairly close U.S.-Iran cooperation in the early stages of the invasion of Iraq were then reinterpreted by the Islamic radicals as a tactical adjustment to help prevent chaos from spreading to Iran (their greatest fear), rather than the basis of a new beginning to better U.S.-Iran relations,

A number of American neoconservatives and others in 2005 and 2006 talked up the idea of extended military action to "bring democracy to Iran." In addition to a fantasy approach to the military numbers, they do not understand that Iranian popular sympathy for the Islamic Republic is weak, but does *not* go to the extent of welcoming aggressive U.S. intervention. Iranians are still deeply sensitive and offended by U.S. support for the Shah in 1953 and up to the revolution.

Ahmed Chalabi, former Deputy Prime Minister of Iraq
Source: Wikipedia, Photo by Michael Gross

The 2005 announcement that the U.S. government was ready to spend $85 million to fund invited proposals from Iran's educational institution, humanitarian groups, nongovernmental organizations, and individuals inside Iran to "support the advancement of Democracy and human rights" through the Iran Liberation Act was rejected in the harshest language. This is the sort of well-intentioned but misguided U.S. congressional effort that increases Iranian official fears, but offers scant payback for the U.S. No funds will ever be disbursed within Iran, and to give them to exile groups here and elsewhere is hardly a prudent use of public resources, as our infatuation with Ahmad Chalabi in Iraq showed.[11] Common sense should tell us that if we often support our country, right or wrong, other nations are likely to do so as well, especially if they are threatened. Such detrimental activities cause Iranians to question our motives and distrust our diplomatic efforts, and they should probably be quietly abandoned.

Perhaps fortunately, those who urge military confrontation with the Iranian regime are faced with a discouraging situation: there are not enough U.S. military forces available to carry out such a policy in the face of strong popular nationalist feeling within Iran. My own reading of this problem over the past decade indicates that there is also near-zero support in the U.S. for reinstituting the military draft to beef up our forces for such a purpose, which is what would be required to consider such an option seriously in the medium term.

With respect to narrower measures, such as an attack on Iran's nuclear program, the possibilities are even more disturbing— Iran has built its program in such a way to give it *three* separate streams to enrich uranium. Even *if* the U.S. had the troops and equipment to take on such an adversary—which it does *not* now have—a raid that failed to eliminate all its capability (and we're not even certain we know where it all is) could end up provoking the attack we fear. It would leave the Iranians with nuclear weapons obtained elsewhere, a raging hatred of the U.S. for attacking them, plus contacts with a number of terrorist groups who could help them smuggle bombs into the U.S. Such an attack would also leave our forces in Iraq vulnerable to even more massive irregular attacks—the Iranians would seek destruction of U.S. forces on Iraq in revenge for significant military action against their soil— that is their pattern.

Analysis and common sense both tell us that there are no military options that do not open up a world of regional hurt for the U.S., or that guarantee Iran would make and keep an agreement to take nuclear weapons out of the equation. The choice of options here goes beyond the question of our relations with Iran, and directly to the heart of the strategy we want to use in foreign affairs generally and the Middle East specifically.

Beyond that, it is clear that coming so soon after our thrust into Iraq, a full U.S. invasion of Iran without European support would bring America's reputation even closer to zero in the Middle East than it has been in the recent past, and further alienate our allies. It would undoubtedly also stimulate terrorism significantly across the region and elsewhere. A late 2004 war game suggested a full-scale invasion of Iran would leave America stuck in a much more dangerous position in Iran than in Iraq—even if we had sufficient forces to do it.[12] Common sense and good judgment suggest, as most serious studies of the problem have, that our only real option is intensive, serious diplomacy, with force a background option.

There are also important, sound and cogent strategic reasons not to enter the tar pit of all-out military action in Iran. Broader issues of who we are as a people suggest that while a strategy of "bringing democracy to the Middle East by force" may sound good to some, it is really in fact well beyond our capacity to accomplish and not what we really want to do. It is certainly not what others in the Middle East want us to do, and to them and to many of our allies, such efforts smack of arrogance and hubris, rather than sound, well-reasoned judgment.

Those pushing unilateral exercise of American power today often suggest we should adopt such a policy because we are the primary world power, the hegemon. We may have primacy, but we are *not* all-powerful. To behave as if we are all-powerful risks losing what we have. That doesn't mean we should never act alone—we have done so often—but that should not be our preferred option. Our diplomacy has been much more successful over the years than people generally realize, but not because we have forced others to accept our political views. Especially with respect to Iran, insisting on doing it our way all the time will lead us into imperial temptations, which will be costly in treasure, blood and reputation. It also goes completely against the grain of our long-term regional interests in the Middle East. Unilaterally posturing effectively removes the vital weapons of diplomacy from our arsenal and leaves us dependent on force—not the best weapon to either bring or teach democracy.

Moreover, from the standpoint of practical capability, our track record in accomplishing specified objectives with force has been at best poor since 2003, and hardly suggests we are ready to take on a battle-prepared nation like Iran, let alone complex issues of development in Iraq. We went into Iraq with too few forces to do the job, no plans for the occupation, and very little support from others. We have borne the burden ourselves to the tune of $400 billion to date. Contrast that with the $6 billion *surplus* the first President Bush received from our allies when the first Gulf War ended. We are overextended and endangering our economic well being, and promoting rather than diminishing terrorism.

With respect to Iran, the choices are hard, but not impossible. With so may Iranians already supportive of democracy and time on their side, a waiting game with minimal threat will enable our potential allies in Iran to grow stronger without having to bear the brunt of being associated with us. It is certainly appropriate for us to also to keep a strong military force available for unexpected situations and to deter Iranian adventurism.

Containment of Iran and offshore balancing forces near the Persian Gulf in the post-Iraq period will, in the long run, do more for our overall security in the Middle East than military action in either Iraq or Iran will do. It will also free our forces to fight terrorism or deal with other challenges more effectively when needed.

SOME U.S. OPTIONS

There are other options that would be worthwhile to examine and keep in mind over the next few years.

A 2004 Council of Foreign Relations (CFR) study on Iran[13] suggested that selective engagement of some form is the only real answer. Efforts at dialog should continue, if only to keep in contact with those who are less hostilely disposed to us.

- The U.S. should keep pressure on the International Atomic Energy Agency (IAEA) to keep an eye on Iran's nuclear program.

- We should continue to have a dialog with those who want it. Drop calls for regime change and installing democracy— let the Iranians do this themselves.

- The U.S. government should be more flexible on sanctions. Trade is the only weapon we can offer, and it benefits our potential allies in Iran far more than our enemies. Moreover, it will create problems for an economic system that is barely able to function in the modern world. It will push Iran into the world trading economy, allow its citizens contact with the world, and diminish radical fundamentalism.

- Allow U.S. nongovernmental organizations to go to Iran, to help with teaching, medical work, etc. Let those who like us in Iran press their government for this. Encourage others from friendly countries to help. This is the best way to help develop democracy.

- Press the Iranians on the status of Al Qaeda prisoners they hold, and be willing in exchange to defang or disband the Iranian exile groups in Iraq who target Iran, but are deeply discredited because of their links with Saddam recently and Marxism previously.

- Continue to keep the heat on the Syrians to leave Lebanon alone—thus narrowing Iran's access to this area.

- Closely monitor Iran's intelligence activities in Iraq. Iraq is an area where our interests should converge more than they diverge—as long as we know what they're doing.

While the CFR group does not talk of reestablishing U.S. diplomatic relations with Tehran, many believe that would be the outcome if we could selectively engage Iran. CFR member and *Newsweek* magazine foreign editor Fareed Zakaria even suggests that President Bush publicly offer to open an embassy in Tehran and begin student exchanges.[14] This would very likely put the hardliners on the defensive—either they accept contact with the world that will eventually diminish their power, or they would be blamed for Iran's economic failures.

Even a principal (and earliest) neoconservative group, The Committee on the Present Danger (CPD), wants the U.S. to be more forward, also suggesting that we offer to reestablish relations with Tehran, to keep the pressure on. CPD even suggests a dialog with Iran's Supreme Jurist about getting the clerics out of politics and returning them to the mosques. This last, along with aid offers to help democracy, are fanciful thinking, but the Committee's call for increased TV and radio programming does make sense in terms of restoring American capacity to affect the opinions of others, which has been seriously degraded over the past twenty years.[15]

Peaceful initiatives have not borne much fruit over the years, nor led to a more substantial dialog that might reduce general hostilities—as happened with Russia during the Cold War. Yet the nuclear issue has generated much discussion in both countries and even though a majority of Iranians now support acquiring nuclear weapons for the first time ever, even such a prestigious individual as Hojatolla Rafsanjani suggested that nuclear weapons might be more dangerous than valuable.

Serious public diplomacy, if it began with less contentious subjects, could lead in time to a broader easing of conflict between

Iran and the rest of the world. Even conservative radical hard-liners, President Ahmadinejad and key foreign policy leaders such as the head of the Supreme National Security Council Ali Larijani have spoken approvingly of Iran's better relations with its Gulf neighbors. For years they maintained a hostile approach to them, and changed only after hostility proved unhelpful to their own interests. In time, the same would happen with the rest of the world.

It is also important to lift our eyes from today's problems to the future. The present regime in Tehran is not likely to outlive its current clerical leadership, since the young are solidly against radical ayatollah-ism. Iran is basically an economic disaster—the impact of which has been masked by the steep rise in oil prices, which has enabled the ayatollahs to spend to survive. If Iran maintains its nuclear inflexibility, the economic consequences of sanctions will increasingly erode, if not destroy, the radical hard-liners' position.

With respect to Iran, our choices are hard, but not impossible. With so may Iranians already supportive of democracy, and more and more religious figures calling for the clergy to quit active politics, time is on the side of those who seek freedom.

Looking further toward politics, some talk of a "grand bargain," in which the U.S. and Iran would basically negotiate all their differences—Tehran would limit its nuclear program to power generation with IAEA inspection, and the U.S. would give Iran security guarantees against an American attack. Both would collaborate to remove terrorists from Iraq and Afghanistan, and recognize each other's interests, as they did in the months following 9/11.

In the diplomatic world of careful preparations, such things do not happen overnight. Selective engagement is needed on problems that can be worked through to build the trust to make the compromises required to take the giant steps. Even some neoconservative "hawks" are realizing that this option offers a better way than involving our overextended military in additional unneeded danger.[16]

A longer, broader view of Iran even more clearly points down the road of diplomacy and patience. Although it's true that the overthrow of Iraq's Saddam Hussein removed one of Tehran's greatest enemies, and Iran is selling its oil to China and having some success with the Hezbollah in Lebanon, matters are not all that bright for Tehran's rulers. They are still surrounded by those the regime considers hostile (including Al Qaeda and especially the Taliban).

Iran's oil industry, deprived of equipment and trained petroleum engineering, is losing ground. High oil prices have hidden declining production, and Iran's oil industry, if not in a "death spiral," is at least in serious decline. The shortage of goods in Iran has been a continuing major source of irritation among Iranians. Even some mainstream Shia clerics are saying in public that it is time for the ayatollahs to return to their mosques. In sum, the picture in Iran is not as bleak as the American right makes it out, nor as ready for immediate and close ties as some on the American left would imagine.

Finally, Americans need to place Iran in the context of our country's broader interests—peace, trade and development. Here, our national interest finds a kindred resonance in the Iranian people. Why go to the extreme of war when time is almost certain to push things our way if we are patient?

As an American Foreign Service officer, I served in Iran before, during and after the 1979 revolution, departing in July before the November 1979 hostage crisis. If I were to speak to some of the radical clerics and younger revolutionaries I got to know during those months, I would suggest that they have blown a great opportunity. Because they failed to adapt their ideas to Persian culture, they have created dislike, distrust and hatred across the

Iranian political spectrum. Unless they change their ways, they are likely to meet the same sad end as past theocratic experiments—demise in violence and bloody revolution. To the degree that they seek to maintain their power by constant reference to the "Great Satan," they are alienating Iran's future generations.

In all fairness, my Iranian interlocutors would probably have a list of grievances and suggestions for me, along the lines Iranian President Ahmadinejad presented to Columbia University in his celebrated and highly criticized speech on September 24, 2007. Such arguments, though, should not get in the way of both countries' greater strategic interest in peace.[17]

Over the past seventy years, American-Iranian relations have run the gamut from love to hate. Careful judgment and calculation of our national interest require us to set this aside. Our policy should be balanced—radical moderation for the longer term, selective collaboration in the short run, and appropriate limited punishments for transgressions against good international order as they occur. This would be consistent with our values and our broad strategic interests. We have no imperial mandate and the overwhelming majority of us do not seek one. Common sense and good judgment strongly suggest that Iran is a really, really good and necessary place to restart our diplomacy.

---

[1] Pollack, Ken. *The Persian Puzzle: The Conflict between Iran and America.* (New York: Random House, 2004), p. 424.

[2] Takeyh, Ray. *Hidden Iran: Paradox and Power in the Islamic Republic,* (New York: Times Books, 2006). This offers the best current analysis of Iran's internal power structure and how the Country relates to the rest of the world.

[3] Stempel, John D. *Inside the Iranian Revolution,* (Bloomington: Indiana University Press, 1981) offers an inside look at how this evolved on the ground in Iran. Sick, Garry. *All Fall Down.* (London: I. B. Tauris, 1985) covers the same ground from a Washington perspective.

[4] Bowden, Mark. *Guests of the Ayatollah.* (New York: Atlantic Monthly Press, 2006) is the most comprehensive recent book on this event.

[5] Takeyh, op. cit., p. 44.

[6] Wright. Robin. *The Last Great Revolution: Turmoil and Transformation in Iran.* (New York: Alfred A. Knopf, 2000) describes the turmoil of the Khatami period extremely well.

[7] MacFarquhar, Neil. "How Iran's Leader Keeps the West off Balance." *The New York Times,* December 13, 2006, p. wk 5.

[8] This military information is taken from the best unclassified source, Cordesman, Anthony H. *Iran's Developing Military Capabilities.* (Washington: The CSIS Press, 2005).

[9] http://ctstudies.com/Document/iran_intel_lopez.html, presentation on Iranian intelligence by Prof. Clare M. Lopez, July 10, 2007, pp. 1-2. There is considerable controversy over Iran's exact role in all of these bombings, but if aid to Hezbollah and even indirectly to Al Qaeda is considered, Iran played at least a supporting role in all of them.

[10] Those who wish to pursue this in detail are urged to read Chubin, Shahram. *Iran's Nuclear Ambitions.* (New York: Carnegie Endowment for International Peace, 2006).

[11] Azimi, Negar. "Hard Realities of Soft Power," *The New York Times Magazine,* June 24, 2007, pp. 50-55.

[12] Fallows, James. "Will Iran be Next?" *The Atlantic,* December 2004, vol. 294, pp. 97-111.

[13] Council on Foreign Relations. *Iran: Time for a new Approach: Report of an Independent Task Force Sponsored by the Council on Foreign Relations,* (New York: Council on Foreign Relations, 2004).

[14] Zakaria, Fareed. "What Iranians Least Expect," *Newsweek,* Oct. 20, 2006.

[15] *Forging an Iran Strategy,* American Foreign Policy Council (Wheaton, IL, Aug. 15, 2006).

[16] Murphy, Dan. "U.S. hawks see strikes on Iran as less likely now," The *Christian Science Monitor,* March 18, 2007, p. 4.

[17] Cooper, Helene. "Ahmadinejad, at Columbia, Parries and Puzzles," *The New York Times,* September 25, 2007, p. 1.

CHAPTER 7
DIPLOMACY & ORGANIZATION

There have only been four truly great organizations in the history of the world—the Roman Empire, the Christian Church, the German Army and Standard Oil of New Jersey.

—Prof. Dwight Waldo

ORGANIZATIONAL COMPETENCE HAS A GREAT DEAL TO do with the effectiveness of policy/decision making. None of the organizations noted in the quote above was a diplomatic establishment: all had cohesive leadership, direct hierarchical leadership, geographical centralization, and a stable environment— qualities seldom found in democratic or even non-democratic foreign affairs establishments.

American government itself rarely has all those qualities, and then historically only in wartime. Any attempt to apply common sense to foreign policy has to account for the nation's capability to define what it wants to do, as well as its ability to "think straight" about international relations. Good individual judgment often depends as much on excellent organizational work as it does on individual effort.

The State Department functions as the foreign ministry of the U.S. and suffers from its crucial role as the principal organizational interlocutor between the U.S. and the rest of the world. It gets blamed for bringing the president bad, or at least unwelcome news; and often has to pass on the same to other countries. To a slightly different degree, the American intelligence community faces the same problems. Insofar as the Defense Department and the Armed Services perform diplomatic functions, the same organizational issues affect them, with the additional problem of coordination with the diplomats.[1]

The career Foreign Service of the United States provides the trained, professional manpower for our diplomatic establishment, and its personnel are also assigned to other related agencies. The secretary of state and his immediate deputies are political appointees from diverse backgrounds. In theory, the secretary of state is the president's closest personal advisor; in practice, it is usually a struggle between the secretary of state and other officials—usually the president's national security advisor and whichever cabinet official has a different view of a problem—the secretary of defense, treasury or commerce.

The State Department deals with over 190 nation-states, many with totally different cultural understandings, most of whom are friendly, but a few of whom are hostile. The U.S. diplomatic establishment has people stationed at over 200 points abroad ranging from embassies to UN observer stations. The Foreign Service largely succeeds in its goal of building a core of experts who specialize in the politics, economics and cultures of the various nation-states, but it is often under fire from politicians, who find it easier to blame the State Department than the president or the policy. How effective these individuals are, however, depends upon a multitude of organizational factors.

The State Department, like any foreign ministry, is challenged by all of the parameters mentioned at the beginning of this chapter, more so because it deals with all of the problems:

Cohesive leadership—is controlled by the president, but often challenged by congress and other government departments.

Direct Hierarchical Leadership—only where and when there is little or no internal conflict over policy.

Geographical centralization and a stable environment—with posts spread all over the world in culturally different environments, this makes life interesting and challenging for Foreign Service personnel, but more complex and difficult to operate with efficiency and effectiveness.[2]

Too often the tendency is to "shoot the messenger," and disparage the State Department, especially if the news is unpleasant or unwanted. This produces a peculiar love/hate relationship between Americans and their diplomats. Former Undersecretary of State David D. Newsom put it nicely:

> The American view of diplomacy is a mixture of ignorance of its details, suspicion of its objectives, contempt for its importance and fascination with its romance. Diplomats are, in the worst of times, considered disloyal, and in the best of times, "cookie pushers." Presidents are traditionally distrustful of the Department of State—which houses diplomats. In no other major country are ambassadorships considered a primary form of political patronage. The risks of death of diplomats in recent years have only partially altered this view.[3]

As a diplomat for twenty-three years, occasionally in unfriendly territory, criticism was rarely directed at me personally, even when I spoke on controversial topics (Vietnam or forbearance in the Middle East). Even for the past two decades as a retired diplomat, I have received the utmost personal respect while occasionally hearing the harshest possible criticisms of the organization to which I once belonged.

In general, however, the State Department thus tends to become the organizational symbol of whatever is perceived wrong with American policy at a given time, even though there are often many officers within it arguing heatedly and persuasively for the very policies that critics are seeking. Once a decision is made, though, officers accept it and either "live to fight another day" or, if the issue is too grave for them, resign. As officials they work better when there is a general consensus on policy, but they are free to express their views before decisions are made.

The absence of a solid basic consensus on foreign policy creates difficulty for policy makers and serious experts who are putting forth their best efforts regardless of the political party in control of the government. It requires a very high order of effective leadership to avoid politicizing the policy process. To politicize this process further into the bureaucracy carries extreme risk to the country as well as to individual careers. When people are "punished" for arguing the "wrong" side of an issue, then "yes-men" dominate, and matters go swiftly awry. Intelligence is shaped to fit leaders' views, and the way is open to turn error into folly (see Chapter 3).

This has frequently been an issue, especially since our involvement in Vietnam fractured the general American bipartisan foreign policy consensus that reigned from 1945 until the late 1960s. It has grown to new and deplorable heights over the past five years since debate began in earnest on U.S. foreign policy in Iraq and the Middle East. As Republican neoconservatives became dominant in the Bush administration, they began to attack the State Department. The centerpiece of this was an article by Newt Gingrich entitled "Rogue State Department," in *Foreign Policy* magazine in the summer of 2003.[4]

Asserting that the State Department has "abdicated values and principles in favor of accommodation and passivity," Gingrich sought to exclude Foreign Service officers from senior departmental positions to allow more political control by the president. The result was a major effort to "promote freedom and combat tyranny," as opposed to concentrating on diplomacy and dealing with others. In other words, the State Department was pressed to become an arm of American primacy, putting forth the President's values without much regard for the situation, their impact on other countries, or their impact on foreign relations.

Newt Gingrich, former Speaker of the U. S. House of Representatives
Source: Wikipedia, Biographical Directory of the U.S. Congress

Gingrich criticized the State Department's Bureau of Intelligence and Research (INR) for issuing a classified intelligence report that stated "liberal Democracy would be difficult to achieve in Iraq" as evidence that the State Department was "disloyal" to the president's policy of providing self-government for Iraq.

In this case, State INR was correct—it was not challenging the president's policy. It was reporting on conditions, not advocating a policy. As it happened, events proved the report correct. If it had been heeded, it might have led to an easing of our discomfort and pain in Iraq. In this case, as in many others, State INR has been correct when the rest of the intelligence community has been wrong—or had its analysis reshaped to fit political vision and hope, as in the case of the CIA's reporting on Iraq's missing weapons of mass destruction.

In this instance and in others, Gingrich and the neoconservatives resolved the clash between external reality and internal neoconservative ideology in favor of the ideology in their own minds. In the long run, this is a recipe for national disaster in both the diplomatic and intelligence organizations. It has been at the heart of our current national difficulties in the Middle

East. Chapters 2 and 3 show how this played out in the conflict with Iraq—specialists were discounted, and hope prevailed over analysis in the decision to invade Iraq, as well as subsequent failure to plan for the event.

Such slanted information is highly destructive of good judgment. For the U.S., the clash between ideological thinking and accurate reporting is a critical organizational issue for diplomacy and judgment at all levels. This is especially true now that we have a single Director of National Intelligence who is mandated to pull it all together. Unless this individual possesses the necessary psychology to bring different views to leaders' attention, we will be handicapped as we begin seeking solutions for even more difficult and complex problems—the future of China, nuclear proliferation efforts of Iran and North Korea, and especially, religiously motivated terrorism. It would be better to allow organizations such as the State Department's INR bureau, the Defense Intelligence Agency and the National Security Agency to have an opportunity to present dissent to key national leaders if their views differ from those of the CIA and the Director of National Intelligence. Only self-confident leaders can make that happen.

INTELLIGENCE AND DEFENSE

Similar organizational stumbling blocks affect the American intelligence community. While they are not charged with managing relations between countries, our intelligence agencies' activities are important in two ways—fostering contact and collaboration with other countries, and our clandestine seeking to uncover the "family jewels" of other nation's secrets. For example, our failure to heed intelligence warnings about the 2005-6 resurgence of the Taliban, following the administration's earlier dismissal of the request for additional troops to complete the destruction of Al-Qaeda at Tora Bora in 2002, set back our battle against terrorism substantially.[5] "We are making more terrorists than we are killing" is the common expression for this serious outcome, and we are currently having to undertake a major effort to strengthen our capability in Afghanistan to catch up.

It is not clear that the intelligence reforms of 2004 have improved the situation or simply centralized the problem under a new intelligence czar. Years ago, Columbia professor Richard K. Betts noted that every reform lays the seeds of errors in the opposite direction (if you insist on a comprehensive report, you may not get it on time; if you refuse to work with any but the morally pure, you will get neither the access to people nor the information that you need). Betts advocated a balanced approach that did not go too far toward either extreme, and also suggested that intelligence errors are endemic, and that comprehensive balance may be the best way to minimize future errors.[6]

Serious similar issues have plagued the defense department. My discussions with a number of serving military people confirmed that pressures exist from key figures on the civilian side of the Defense Department upon the military forces to produce material illustrating positive results. Along with that comes an unwillingness to hear reporting that goes against the expectations of the policy—in this case, the suppression of insurgent groups in Iraq, and the expanding civilian chaos there and in Afghanistan.

The issue is a little more complex with the military, because the "can-do" mentality that is essential for effective combat leadership does not encourage officers to put forward negative assessments. Careers suffer as a result if they do, and only senior officers who are willing to dig will get at the truth. There are many who do, however—and then the question becomes: Will the information be passed on to civilian leadership and shared with the rest of the international relations community?

Chapter 2 outlined the result General Shinseki encountered when his estimate of the forces needed to conquer and pacify

General Eric Ken Shinseki, former Chief of Staff of the U.S. Army

Source: www.defenseimagery.mil, photo by Scott Davis

Iraq were more than double those of his boss, the secretary of defense. He was summarily retired, the U.S. went on into Iraq with too few forces to do the job, and further discussion of additional troops has been a touchy subject even since. The American political culture of civilian control of the military has stood our nation well. We have not, however, developed a process for dealing with situations where the civilians are way off the mark. As one senior military officer put it to me. "The military services are becoming stressed over what their proper behavior is when the civilians are the ones who are nuts."[7]

Getting correct information and making astute assessments are even more complex when they involve different cultures and different conceptions of politics—as most all foreign problems do. There is a premium in all organizations for people who are knowledgeable about such problems and wise and experienced enough to see through these cultural issues. In the military, Foreign Area Studies officers are the equivalent of State Department area experts—and often have the same problems of being heard at higher command levels. Such people, in my experience, often have an uncommon amount of knowledge, but that in turn is often unappreciated by those of an ideological, preconceived bent, and thus frequently fail to advance our policy objectives.

A related issue involves the adequacy of the National Security Council (NSC), headed by the President's Special Assistant for National Security Affairs, currently Stephen Hadley. Since its inception in 1947, it has been the group that brings input for all departments together to insure that work is being done to meet the president's needs.[8] Under high profile leaders such as Walt

Rostow in the Johnson Administration or Henry Kissinger in the Nixon Administration, the NSC made policy itself. Under more organizationally focused individuals, the NSC served basically as an information manager, making sure the president saw everyone's views. The present head seems to be following this latter pattern as well. My own impression of history is that the council works best in this mode. However, it is not clear whether the NSC in its present form is fully adequate for the present complexities which involve a great deal more that merely the traditional view of "national security."[9]

The next national administration would do well to assess the council in terms of its mission and usefulness in the present environment.

GROUPTHINK

Chapter 3 highlighted "groupthink," situations in which policy/decision-makers focused on a very narrow range of possibilities for action. The Bay of Pigs disaster in 1961 was an example of successive mistakes being made because no one asked the hard questions about the plan to invade Cuba—a plan that had been handed over to the Kennedy Administration by the outgoing Eisenhower team. The next year, lessons learned from the 1961 event were crucial to preventing the same kind of "groupthink," from driving the response to Soviet efforts to install missiles in Cuba.[10] We have yet to see a similar exercise at the federal level on issues stemming from the Iraq war.

People want to please their bosses, and in most "groupthink" studies, results show that a senior individual who is not willing to entertain dissenting ideas will soon not have any placed before him. The story of recent American foreign relations confirms that to be the case. President Bush himself has remained stubbornly attached to policies that are not working in the face of reporting from within the American government, including his first

Secretary of State, Colin Powell. As a result, people have been promoted for stubbornness in defense of policies, not concern for the truth.[11] This goes against common sense and is the most effective way to skew judgment to the nation's detriment.

Organizational issues

Other issues affect the flow of government as well. The foreign affairs function has been chronically short of funding since the early 1970s. Recruitment for the Foreign Service dropped significantly in the early 1990s. Embarrassing and stressful initially, it became a critical problem later in the 1990s, eased only by Colin Powell's strong insistence in 2002 that the State Department receive sufficient budgetary resources and start hiring enough officers to fill substantial vacancies in the Foreign Service. State is still short of personnel to fulfill its assignments under current counterinsurgency planning for Iraq and Afghanistan.

That has not kept the State Department from being the most studied organization in government. Over the past sixty years, more that twenty significant studies have been conducted about the State Department and the Foreign Service. These include major in-house efforts in 1970 and 2000 by the department itself.

The principal reason why money has always been short is that until 2007 the State Department, unlike the Defense Department and the Intelligence Community, has not been considered to be behind the national security budget "firewall," which protects it from serious challenge. It is now, in 2007, for the first time behind the firewall.[12] Previously state's appropriations were not considered in the federal budget as national security matters; the department competed with domestic departments, including Justice and Commerce, for its budgetary allocations. As the only federal agency without a specific domestic constituency (Defense has contractors; Agriculture has farmers, Commerce has businessmen, etc.), State has been at a distinct organizational disadvantage when it comes to seeking funding to maintain and strengthen our diplomatic presence. This is particularly hurtful when the administration keeps demanding a more activist foreign policy.

Our diplomats abroad are spread too thin in many places, and our aid and public diplomacy outreach suffers as well. The folding of the Agency for International Development (AID) and the United States Information Agency (USIA) back into the State Department in the late 1990s has significantly reduced our organizational capacity to extend and manage foreign assistance and deliver America's story persuasively.[13] Money is tighter and functions have been reduced. Politically, we spend a lot for war and too little for peace. It remains to be seen if the new posture adopted in 2007 will increase the needed resources consistently over several years.

Unless the U.S. pays more attention to its Foreign Service personnel in terms of training and family service conditions abroad, our diplomatic service will deteriorate rapidly. Streamlining the examination process would boost the recruiting of top candidates. Unless it pays serious attention to these organizational needs, the Service will not attract the most capable people. Such issues continue to stir professional concern within the foreign affairs community.[14]

There is no fundamental reason why the public diplomacy and foreign assistance activities can not function as well under State Department control as they did as separate agencies, but in practice they also have tended to suffer from the tight budgetary restrictions facing the State Department. When AID and USIA were independent organizations, they had their own links with Congress. If they remain within the State envelope, they will need to have high-profile leaders with the political clout to gather the organizational sway they clearly need.

Even during the Cold War years, the State Department was consistently undermanned. America was growing into a major power, but with a very small, non-career diplomatic service. As late as 1910, there were only 1,277 officers and staff personnel to serve 48 embassies and 324 consulates (mostly one-man posts). Even after the enactment of the Rogers Act creating the modern foreign service in 1924, the service remained small. In 1940, on the eve of World War II, only 1,968 foreign service personnel ran 312 posts and staffed several State Department positions.

In 1950, foreign service personnel peaked at 16,319 for 74 countries, a figure that dipped as low as thirteen thousand by 1970, and was not reached again until 1990, and then only briefly. Soon after that, the number of nations reached 180, climbing to 184 countries to monitor by 2004. 2006 saw 11, 397 Foreign Service personnel in service,[15] matched against much greater action requirements in Iraq and Afghanistan as well as additional problems in the rest of the world, which generate more public diplomacy and assistance work.

Mike Mansfield, former U.S. Senator and Senate Majority Leader
Source: Wikipedia, by Aaron Shikler, Oil on canvas

This personnel stretch left the State Department with minimal links to other, larger government agencies as well as inadequate ties to other foreign affairs groups in the U.S.—private aid organizations, religious development programs and academic cohorts. As late as the early 1970s the department used to bring in thirty university faculty members once or twice a year and assign them to work alongside departmental officials for two to three weeks. This arrangement benefited everyone—the professors got to see the "real world," their State Department colleagues got to sample the work academics were doing. Mutual understanding developed that was useful on both sides in coping with future problems.

Another issue, exceptionally complex, is the question of the size and construction of our foreign missions. As late as the 1960s, it was very rare for an embassy to be attacked, damaged or destroyed. Traditional diplomatic immunity held sway, and as our overseas foreign presence grew, American embassies and cultural centers were built to be open to visitors. That changed with the onset of terrorism and diplomatic kidnapping, beginning the late 1960s and escalating through the 1970s.

Newer buildings have had more security, but less access, and the size of some missions is becoming both a security and political issue. The new U.S. Embassy in Baghdad will be the world's largest and most expensive foreign mission covering 104 acres (our own White House occupies 18 acres), and cost $592 million. It was designed for a full American presence and based on the hope that central Baghdad, where it is located, would see an end to random political violence. Creating this huge enclave has severely limited both construction and repair money for other missions, a result which degrades our overall capabilities elsewhere.[16] The huge size of the mission also creates problems of finding adequate staff, when our needs suddenly grow as they did in Iraq. [17]

At a more general level, the relationship between political appointees and career officers is another area of concern. Some "politicals" are knowledgeable and others are not. Some have common sense and good judgment, and some do not. Similarly, some career people work better than others with political appointees. The U.S. is the only country that uses political appointees, regardless of qualification, extensively as ambassadors, This not infrequently includes a substantial contribution to the president's political party.[18] The results are mixed—some outstanding political appointees such as ambassadors David Bruce, Robert Goheen, Mike Mansfield and Elliot Richardson spring to mind, but for every one of those, there have been appointees who could not even name the principal cities or the

Elliot Richardson, Ambassador to Great Britain and only four-time U.S. cabinet officer

Source: Department of Commerce Photographic Services

chief of state of the country to which they were being assigned—and this at their nomination hearings! Lacking this and other basic knowledge, their judgment is often marginal.

Common sense—and good judgment—suggests that this practice should be sharply reduced. Political candidates should at the very minimum pass review by a presidential board that has both political and career foreign service individuals as members. My former colleague, the late Prof. Vince Davis and I twice proposed training sessions for new political officials in the State Department, but the sensitivities apparently outweighed the expected utility—though many both there and elsewhere thought such seminars would improve the functions both of the State Department and intra-governmental coordination efforts.

Another perennial issue relating to organizational effectiveness is the debate over whether foreign service personnel and others working in this area should be hired and promoted for their general overall expertise, or whether they should have extensive area and regional qualifications. Foreign Service personnel are hired for worldwide availability but many acquire special training and expertise—language and cultural understanding—in a particular country (Russia, China or India) or a region (The Middle East, Latin America or Western Europe). Before you can consult regional experts, you have to find or grow them, and then actually consult them. The U.S. has been deficient in both hiring and promoting, and finds itself extremely short-handed in Middle Eastern expertise. This issue needs continued, timely attention. The best solution, of course, would be to balance the two, but often needs grow much faster than they can be supplied. Perceptive thought and judgment will also try to minimize this sort of organizational issue.

In fact, effective organizations with well-trained folks that can shape well-considered policies can magnify the country's effectiveness substantially. The world often considers Americans masters of organization, but too often we ourselves continue to hold on to the charms of individuality—the old Horatio Alger myth, updated most recently by Microsoft's Bill Gates. Organizations can acquire more knowledge more rapidly, master dealings with different cultures, train the next generation, and put individuals into the field with resources to meet challenges.

Such organizations are indispensable in a complex world for carrying out broad policies and helping set and achieve significant goals. (Even Bill Gates has helpers!) Poorly led, with unrealistic goals, an organization may still be able to limit damage if it maximizes employee effectiveness. This holds true for all three elements of the national security triad: diplomacy, defense and intelligence. This will not happen, of course, if the policies are skewed, the resources are inadequate, and good leadership is lacking. Diplomacy is more likely to succeed if its efforts are in the service of well grounded, realistic, balanced and common sense strategies generated by statesmen and managed by competent individuals, not ideologues.

It takes strong, sensible leadership to manage organizations and prevent conflict between two or more of them from crippling the policy process. Such leadership can only be effective in a democracy if it rallies people in support of values that command widespread majority support for national strategy and goals. The past five years in the U.S. have seen that process hijacked by small groups of individuals with a very narrow ideological focus and limited knowledge of reality in the world. Often they are also under inadequate supervision. Putting such pressure on our professional military, our diplomats, and our intelligence officers has led to both error and organizational ineffectiveness as truth has been suppressed and reality ignored. If this happens continuously, the international environment can be extremely unforgiving, even (or perhaps *especially*) for a superpower.

Perhaps this is best illustrated by the story of two stable boys cleaning the stalls. William said to his much larger friend Joe: "Joe, you got horseflies flying 'round your head!" Joe replied, picking up a menacing shovel, "Now, William you know what horseflies gather round and eat—are you insinuating?" William, hastily beating a retreat to the end of the building, said, "No, no, of course not, Joe," then, turning the corner and racing away, added, "but you can't fool them horseflies. . . ."

When it comes to good organizations and good people in foreign affairs, you can't fool those horseflies either.

---

[1] Priest, Dana. *The Mission.* (W.W. North & Co., 2003), esp. chs. 1-3.

[2] These categorizations are my own, but are inspired by the observations of Downs, Anthony. *Inside Bureaucracy.* (Boston, Little, Brown and Co., 1967); as well as other Foreign Service colleagues, 1965-present.

[3] Newsom, David D. *Diplomacy and American Democracy.* (Bloomington: Indiana University Press, 1988), p. 6.

[4] Gingrich, Newt. "Rogue State Department," *Foreign Policy,* No. 137, July/August (2003), pp. 12-48.

[5] Risen, James. *State of War: The Secret History of the CIA and the Bush Administration.* [New York: Free Press, 2006] Chs. 4 and 7; and Coll, Steve. *Ghost Wars: The Secret History of the CIA, Afghanistan and bin Laden, from the Soviet Invasion to September 10, 2001.* (New York: Penguin Books, 2004).

[6] Betts, Richard K. "Analysis, War and Decision: Why Intelligence Failures Are Inevitable," *World Politics, vol.* 31 (October 1978), pp. 61-89. For examples in Iraq, see Seliktar, Ofira. *The Politics of Intelligence and American Wars with Iraq.* (New York: Palgrave Macmillan, 2008), especially ch. 7.

[7] Author's interviews with serving military officers, April 2005, December 2006 and June 2007.

[8] Rothkopf, David J. *Running the World: The Inside Story of the National Security Council and the Architects of America's Power.* (New York: Public Affairs Press, 2005), chs. 1 and 13.

[9] Rothkopf, op. cit., pp. 439-47. Soderberg, Nancy. *The Superpower Myth: The Use and Misuse of American Might.* (New York: John Wiley and Sons, 2005), pp. 87-98 and 247-43.

[10] Janis, Irving. *Groupthink.* (Houghton Mifflin Co., 1985), chs. 2 and 6.

[11] Woodward, Bob. *State of Denial.* [Simon and Schuster, New York. 2006), final three chapters.

[12] U.S. Department of State, Transcript of Secretary of State Condoleezza Rice's remarks in the East Auditorium, Department of State, Washington, D.C., line 14.

[13] Fitzpatrick, Kathy R. "The Collapse of American Public Diplomacy: What diplomatic experts say about rebuilding America's image in the World—a view from the trenches." Unpublished paper from the 2008 International Studies Association Conference.

[14] See the American *Foreign Service Journal,* May 2007, focus issue on "An Uncertain Path Ahead: The Foreign Service As a Career," especially pp. 20-34.

[15] Figures at: http://www.state.gov/s/d/rm/rls/perfrpt/2006/html/76630.htm

[16] Gearan, Ann. "U.S. Embassy Not Safe Enough," *Lexington Herald-Leader,* May 2, 2007, p. 3.

[17] Kessler, Glenn, "Embassy Staff in Baghdad Inadequate," *The Washington Post,* June 19, 2007, p. A1; Wright, Robin. "Stress Taking Toll on Foreign Service," *The Washington Post,* June 20, 2007, p. A17.

[18] Kennedy, Paul, "Embassies for Sale," *The International Herald Tribune,* May 14, 2007, p. 1.

CHAPTER 8

SAFE FOR OUR GRANDCHILDREN

We must look to the rising generation for the restoration of the country.

—Gen. Robert E. Lee, August 1865

GENERAL LEE'S WORDS ARE TRUE TODAY, AND REFLECT THE long strategic view. If we are to have any hope of improving our national capability to increase our knowledge, reduce ideology and improve our judgment about our own foreign affairs successfully, it will have to be a team effort. We need, not necessarily in any specific order: greater citizen awareness; better organization and relations among our citizens; better citizen knowledge about the rest of the world; and a much more well-grounded foreign policy crew. Only

The explosion of the Marine Corps building in Beirut, Lebanon on October 23, 1983 created a large cloud of smoke that was visible from miles away.
Source: Wikipedia, Official USMC Photo

as these develop will we create more competent government to make and carry out policies that reflect values rich enough to gather broad support at home and abroad. We must do this—or else the U.S. will join a historical landscape littered with countries that have failed to manage their global foreign affairs effectively— the most recent being the Soviet Union.

Common sense involves creating balanced and moderate policies and carrying them out in a competent and consistent manner to maximize their effectiveness. Such policies need to be based on and drawn from a country's values. Good judgment is needed to see that important needs are not slighted in favor of merely urgent ones. There is no magic key to ensuring that all will be well, but such policies are more likely to prevail if this is the case. Ideologues are dangerous, especially when they cause the body politic to overlook reason or bend it to their aims and ignore reality in the rest of the world.

It is more difficult for organizations and societies to structure themselves to prevent similar failings without farsighted leadership, well versed in the past and with a keen eye toward the future. For example, the U.S. was involved in fighting insurgencies as early as 1898-1913 and well into the late 1940s and 1950s in Greece, and the Philippines—did we learn from that in Vietnam? Not enough, it seems. We fought insurgencies poorly in Vietnam—did we learn from that in Iraq? No, we put our learning back on the shelf, and error became folly—again.

We have been involved extensively in the Middle East for at least sixty years, yet as a nation we have learned and digested far too little about the different cultures and religions there—or so it appears from some of our present policies. We do not even register properly how others view us, and we find ourselves generally detested in a region that is critical to our prosperity and our direct security. We accept our victory in the Cold War as natural, and discount the reactions of others, leaving us with fewer friends and more enemies as we have focused on American primacy as a goal above all others.

In most cases we fail largely because our societal memory is not good. As World War II veteran and the nation's third Poet Laureate, Howard Nemerov, said before his death in 1991, "The reason we do not learn from history is that we are not the same people who learned the last time."

Both people and leaders have deserted some of the basic tenets of common sense, hoping optimistically, I suppose, that the noted German Chancellor of the nineteenth century, Otto von Bismarck, was correct when he said, "God has a special providence for fools, drunks, and the United States of America."[1] But the more we behave like we think we deserve our success by right—and not God's grace—the less others feel we deserve it, and the less attractive we are to others. Most monarchies learned that the hard way; only a few survive today.

We are living now in Kyraic times, a biblical phrase signifying a period of fundamental change, great emotion and enormous consequences. Major decisions with momentous implications are being made—or put off. Serious failures of our own competence in foreign affairs are occurring. We are having to balance more fundamental issues with urgent contemporary needs. Our political life is in a period of extreme discontent. Others in the world like us less now than at any time in our history, and we don't seem to connect effectively with other nations.[2]

If we review the impediments to common sense and good judgment mentioned in Chapter 1, it is clear that our lack of knowledge about foreign cultures and the ideological rigidity that impedes learning about them has affected us very negatively over the past six years. We have stressed American primacy far too much and focused almost solely on the benefits and not the costs, even as the quality of our lives has become poorer. The vast reservoir of good will that came our way after 9/11 has been squandered. Our citizens know something is wrong, but they have not yet discerned the reasons and come together to correct the problem.

On the positive side, primacy allows U.S. influence and broad flexibility in confronting chaos. It offers significant military benefits and possible alliances. Our size and power give us more control and significant opportunities for lowering currency and economic transaction costs, which produce substantial economic benefits while providing the "glue" for our key international relationships. If managed with care and balance, our position can enable the U.S. to pursue our national interests while contributing to global security.[3]

Negatively, the cost of primacy is trade-offs against the positive goals. The tendency to "imperial overstretch" alienates allies and stimulates opposition to our global power. It encourages others to engage in "soft balancing" (economic and political) against us, and perhaps even eventually "hard balancing" of military power to oppose us. We should accept that primacy is a condition, not a prize, and deal with it more thoughtfully and with less strutting.

The paradox is that primacy's benefits and costs depend on how it is exercised. Our adventure in Iraq has shown that we are not now very competent nor very adept at most aspects of nation building. On a broader scale, diplomacy has slipped into disuse as we have focused on Iraq, Iran and the rest of the Middle East. Our diplomatic and intelligence capacities have atrophied as compared against the tasks we ask them to perform. We simply do not have the cadres of personnel or effective action doctrines for a variety of needed activities such as nation building, humanitarian intervention or insurgent warfare. Moreover, we have almost refused to turn to those who do, particularly international organizations.

We currently treat terrorism as a concrete enemy, not as the tactic it truly is; we emphasize the military response out of proportion to the necessary police and political efforts that would bring in more allied help.[4] We are too focused on the "American Empire" concept.

The militarization of our response to terrorism has diverted our attention, handicapped our diplomacy, multiplied our costs, and left us less flexibility to deal with other serious problems— such as North Korean nuclear weapons and Darfur's humanitarian disaster, not to mention long-range challenges such as AIDS, global warming and potential epidemics that can never be dealt with by any single country.

I believe the weight of evidence, past and contemporary, suggests that democracy and empire are ultimately incompatible, and that our democratic process will ultimately opt to turn away from empire building and reject the "imperial" mission as it struggles to cope with the following problems:[5]

1. The pressure of "imperial necessity" for control, requiring ever greater expenditure and manpower in the face of growing domestic demands (Chapters 1 and 7);

2. Compulsions that corrupt democratic freedoms, such as the pressures to use torture in interrogation (Chapters 5 and 6); and

3. The innate drive for hierarchical military control necessitated by "imperial" activity (Chapters 2, 6 and 7), which tends to curb our democratic freedoms.

The fact of America's strength means that the nation must play a major world role, but that must done in cooperation with others. Some may want her to shrink back into her own borders (which we scarcely control now!). However most, at home *and* abroad, recognize the U.S. as an essential player in the international system. The U.S. was a major player in creating modern multilateral diplomacy through international organizations, and for its own greater good should make much more use of international institutions such as the UN and the World Bank. Domestic pressures will not let America be a classic "empire" in the format of Rome, or even nineteenth century Britain, and none but the extreme fringes in the world want

America to withdraw to our own shores. Nor could we survive in our present form if we did. The vast majority of our citizens oppose this as well, once they understand the pressures and the costs. Not all of our foreign policy elite understand this.

Aside from moments of frustration, what was wrong with the deductive, pragmatic strategy that made the U.S. a leader for over sixty years and counting? It may seem messy, but it worked better than the approach tried in recent years. The strategy we used then was based on common sense understanding of others' attitudes and needs.

The answer for the U.S. is to relearn how to interact more effectively with others, and to focus on the gains of peaceful diplomacy and building a stronger international community. We need to relearn the lesson that we have to build good relationships with as many others as we can. We are already traveling more, and are of necessity more deeply engaged abroad. To most young people sixty years ago, "foreign" meant slipping across the state border to Ohio to get 3.2 beer. Today, many high school and college students routinely travel to experience different cultures; from the Middle East to Central and South Asia, Africa and the Orient. We must find a way to mobilize them, as the Kennedy generation did with returning Peace Corps volunteers in the 1960s and '70s.

Engagement with others abroad requires more and better diplomacy driven by an informed citizenry, so that our natural inclination to make friends can pay dividends in both the public and private spheres. The goal should be a strategy that brings peoples and nations together in cooperation, rather than military adventure.

Understatement, humility, moderation and avoidance of bluster should be the motifs of our diplomatic attitudes. If the U.S. must exercise power effectively even against the wishes of its allies—and there will be such times—it should do so with a bland, mildly regretful smile, not boastful words. The country should pick its fights carefully and divide its enemies, as it is now beginning to do after nearly four years in Iraq.

America would do well to seek balance in its engagement with the world, and make a greater concurrent effort to avoid pursuing error to the point of folly. It is perhaps more difficult for a democracy to change course quickly than it is for a totalitarian society, because it requires changing more people's minds. However, as and when the democracy does shift, it is more effective because it generates more support.

In developing our strategy, diplomacy and military posture, we need to get back to some basics:

1. Make a serious effort to develop a national strategy and foreign policy consensus based on widely accepted values. A small group, such as the neoconservatives, should have to sell its program to the people before it seeks expensive commitments with years of funding required. If the history of the past sixty years is any guide, successful programs/ policies that meet that criterion will almost always turn out to be broader, moderate, balanced and centrist. Politics, as Hal Sunders said, is about relationships. So is good foreign policy, and this includes relations with our friends *and* even our enemies.

2. Stamp out the hubris and arrogance that has infected so much of our foreign policy over the past six years. It doesn't work and it generates greater disdain, hatred and danger to us all, as the continuing rise of Al Qaeda in Iraq and elsewhere has demonstrated.

3. Relearn diplomacy and learn to "play well with others." Former Ambassador Charles Freeman says America currently has, for the first time, "a foreign policy without diplomacy." It's time to move diplomacy to the fore and take it seriously. It has taken the present administration about

six years to even approach this point, but we have ample examples of how it should be done in our own national past if we have the wit and will to explore *and fund* it.

4. Accept and deal with America's democratic attention deficit disorder—difficulty in focusing on long-term goals and allocating sufficient resources for *both* domestic and foreign priorities. Globalization has mixed them up, and as a people, we need to better handle, or at the very least be more humble about, flaws in our own system: failing health care; corporate corruption; and poor/unequal education. We would then be going back to our traditional posture of leading by example. This would also help improve our current standing with others and inspire more cooperation.

Perhaps the most difficult part of rebuilding a national consensus will be integrating appropriate religious values into our policy processes. In the American case, separation of church and state has been one of our key national political myths; both religious belief and religion have played a key role in our own national life. Early Americans saw the U.S. as the "New Jerusalem," the "City Upon a Hill" where people could work out their destinies freed of the old restraints. We were never perfect, but we have, more than most, understood cartoonist Walt Kelly's famous political banner, "We have met the enemy and they is us." Freedom of religion was such a key tenet of our country's early political life that belief in a divine creator suffused our political life—and still does despite the increasing twentieth century secularization of society. We need to be more conscious of this religious/secular balance and its implications for national unity and diplomacy.

Perceptive Council on Foreign Relations scholar Walter Russell Mead has described the resurgence of the evangelical tradition in America over the past fifty years. In 1960 there were two million more Methodists than Baptists, by 2005 there were more Baptists than Methodists, for example. While hard-core Christian fundamentalists have little to say about foreign affairs, the evangelicals and the liberal Protestants are increasingly finding common cause on many issues—the need for increased foreign aid and humanitarian relief, and support for Israel (but not Zionism). The evangelical tradition has a strong background in missionary work, which can help give America a better approach to interfaith dialog. This in turn will be increasingly critical to preventing dangerous religious clashes both across and within national boundaries.[6]

There are dangers as well as opportunities here. The gap between secularists and the religious, and conflicts between religious groups, can often lead to major disagreements and fights, made more difficult by the fact that they are religious and often less amenable to compromise. Nevertheless, the U.S. has balanced this off in the past, and the price for not doing so again is one we will not wish to pay. Where is Reinhold Niebuhr when we need him?

Integrating our religious values will be especially important for this era's major threat: dealing with terrorism. The terrorism we face in the Middle East has religious roots that are not susceptible to being rooted out by military force—at least not without a substantial component of public diplomacy as well as a willingness to win over those now estranged. Greater awareness of the issues is key. We responded inadequately to an attempt by Al Qaeda to take over Somalia in early 2007, and only the intervention of Ethiopia saved the day (Mussolini must be laughing in his grave). We have shown inadequate leadership in stopping the ongoing Darfur tragedy, which has already killed over three hundred thousand people and displaced an additional million or more. Several of our policies in the Middle East over the past four years have played into bin Laden's hands as Al Qaeda tries to convince the Middle East and others of American imperial intentions.

What needs to emerge from all this is a U.S. world-view sufficiently broad and balanced to permit the U.S. to meet the challenges of the coming years. Globalization, the arrival of Thomas Freidman's "Flat World" where wages go steadily down, magnified by globalization of production, poses profound social and political challenges to all nations, but especially to the U.S. Energy issues will get worse, not better, as oil prices continue to go up in the face of steadily growing demand from China and India, whose economies are growing at 10 percent per year. New centers of global power are growing faster than one might have thought two years ago. Bonn, Moscow, Riyadh, Tehran, New Delhi and

SOUTHEAST ASIA

Courtesy of The Universtiy of Texas Libraries, The University of Texas at Austin

Beijing will be driving new economic, scientific and political initiatives, not all of which will meet with our approval or even acceptance. It will be greatly to our advantage if we can develop more sway in these areas.

The answer cannot be a return to isolation—"if you don't do it my way, I'll take my toys and go home." It didn't work in the 1930s and rudimentary common sense tells us it certainly won't work now in the era of globalization. We are too much involved with the world; we are the eight hundred-pound gorilla, for better or worse. While it may be wearing and frustrating, a careful look at our situation shows us it could be a lot worse.

We cannot escape dealing with others—modern communications are all too pervasive, travel too convenient. The Internet is becoming a powerful force both politically and economically. Small numbers of people organizing through the Internet can exert substantial influence over democratic governments—witness the 1997 international campaign to ban landmines, and our own 2006 elections.

The point is to use our capacities and our skill to best advantage to come up with the best solutions to our outstanding issues. If we practice the politics of division and narrow interest, we will limp along like those nations who fail to cope realistically with their own problems. Our unique skill for the past one hundred years has been our pragmatic nature and willingness to use common sense and perseverance. Out of this has often come superior judgment that has brought us to a position of unequaled, but not infinite, power.

The real question is whether we as a people have the focus and willingness to do it. Even the so-called foreign policy elites are in disarray as the administration pulls up its drawbridges and deliberately spurns expertise on many problems. This in turn prevents our organizational entities from being as effective as they could be.

Individually, how to proceed? Keeping track of what's happening currently is a good place the start. For most, information comes from newspapers, television, the occasional book or magazine, plus discussion with others. The bibliography of this book is a comprehensive list of possible readings—check the footnotes on subjects of interest and read them.

For most, the best way to begin would be to check Appendix A for the author's list of seven "must read" books to begin further education. Scan the press; and if you're interested enough and involved, read the Sunday edition of the *New York Times*, or any other major metropolitan newspaper with an international focus.

The next step would be to read at least one good weekly news magazine. My personal choice is The *Economist*, but *Newsweek*, *Time* and *U.S. News and World Report* are all good to superior on international issues. An excellent alternative that mixes the daily press and weekly/monthly offerings is the five-day-a-week mailed edition of the *Christian Science Monitor*. It is very easy to read, clear, and highly informative. In the course of a month, it covers all the areas of the world, with articles on many complex issues.

Next, check out and read articles on topics of interest in the journals *Foreign Affairs* and/or *Foreign Policy*. These can be found at most libraries, and are not as expensive as you might think for a subscription.

If you live near a major metropolitan area or a university city, a little checking will probably turn up university departments, committees on foreign affairs, or UN associations that feature contemporary speakers, many from the policy-making world. You can go as far as you like—we do not all have time to devote the substantial attention to foreign affairs that a professor of international affairs or a Foreign Service Officer does.

Organizationally, you may wish to join the Foreign Policy Association, which offers study guides each year, or specialized organizations such as the Middle East Institute. A list of these can be found in the list of key web sites offered at Appendix B. For those who like to do it themselves, however, build your own collection by putting a subject (Arab-Israeli dispute, NAFTA) in the SEARCH block of Google or any other Internet search engine, and explore what you discover.

A word of warning: do not gravitate exclusively to books or web sites that merely repeat your own views—take a look at what people are saying on *both* sides of an issue before you make up your mind. Both professional magazines noted—*Foreign Affairs* and *Foreign Policy*—frequently have for/against articles on particular policy questions. The Foreign Policy Association has a "Great Decision" program that offers alternative views on eight-ten issues per year.

Let us conclude with a short sketch of objectives we might consider in terms of more specific policies, applying judgment to a common-sense look at our conditions today:

1. Renew our commitment to selective multilateral action as opposed to unilateral moves wherever possible. Strengthen both the size and quality of our representation at the UN and fund it to fight more strenuously to build coalitions. On security issues, we should act with the UN's blessing where possible, but with the support of like-minded allies if not. In the process, examine carefully the full range of problems we have, especially those where little has been done. Seek comprehensive, agreed solutions. They last longer.

2. Avoid reliance on preventive force, defined as taking military action before the decision to strike has been made by a hostile power. Do this by recasting our national strategy and scrapping the 2002 version. Urge both political parties to significantly upgrade our foreign service, economic and humanitarian assistance and public diplomacy infrastructures. Invest in the people and training necessary to do what we want and need to

do abroad. Inadequate organization and skill development can kill the best of intentions. A modest policy well carried out is far preferable and ultimately more successful than a really good policy poorly and unrealistically pushed forward with inadequate resources.

3. Recognize the importance of global public opinion, and strengthen U.S. public diplomacy accordingly. Be mindful that public diplomacy cannot sell policies that deeply offend people. Public relations are no substitute for effective policy, and they can't sell poor policy to people it enrages. Explaining ourselves well is no more costly than doing it badly, but pays much better dividends.

4. Work seriously again toward bipartisanship in American foreign policy. Major issues are too important to play politics with. Others will look to our example and emulate it. We are at our best when we work together.

An informed look at our current situation that stimulates effective action would enable America to deal successfully with the vast majority of our problems. We have much to do in many areas. But we can succeed—if we can show the strength and determination that won World War II, the altruism that achieved a fair peace, and the prudence that achieved a benign end to the Cold War. We will be in a position that is much more realistic, much more congruent with our own values, and more acceptable to others—perhaps even closer to the true "City Upon a Hill" our founding fathers envisioned, and much safer indeed for our children and grandchildren.

---

[1] Quoted in Mead, Walter Russell. *Special Providence: American Foreign Policy and How it Shaped the World.* (Alfred A. Knopf, New York, 2001), p. vii.

[2] Pilon, Juliana Geran. *Why America is Such a Hard Sell: Beyond Pride and Prejudice.* (Rowman & Littlefield, New York, 2007), see especially chs. 2 and 14.

[3] Odom, William and Richard Dujarric. *America's Inadvertent Empire.* (New Haven: Yale Nota Bene, 2005), pp. 204-16.

[4] Priest. *The Mission*, pp. 13 and 390-94.

[5] Pilon, op. cit. pp. 67-69.

[6] Mead, Walter Russell. "God's Country?" *Foreign Affairs*, September/October 2006, vol. 85, no. 5, pp. 24-43.

BIBLIOGRAPHY

Ameringer, Charles D. *U.S. Foreign Intelligence: The Secret Side of American History.* (Lexington: Lexington Books, 1990).

Anonymous (Michael Scheuer). *Imperial Hubris: Why the West is Losing the War on Terror.* (Washington: Brassey's Inc., 2004).

———. *Through Our Enemies' Eyes.* (Washington: Brassey's, Inc., 2002).

Aslan, Reza. *No god but God.* (New York: Random House, 2006).

Azimi, Negar. "Hard Realities of Soft Power," The New York Times Magazine, June 24, 2007, pp. 50-55.

Bacevich, A.J. *American Empire.* (Cambridge: Harvard University Press, 2002).

Baer, Robert. *See No Evil.* (New York: Crown Publishers, 2002).

Bamford, J. *A Pretext for War.* (New York: Doubleday/Random House (2004).

Barry, Tom. A Common Sense Foreign Policy Based on American Values and History (published June 5, 2005 by *Common Dreams,* at Internet site http://www.commondreams.org/cgi-bin/print. cgi?file=/views05/0605-27.htm.

Betts, Richard K. "Analysis, War and Decision: Why Intelligence Failures Are Inevitable," *World Politics* 31 (October 1978), 61-89.

———. *Conflict After The Cold War: Arguments On Causes Of War And Peace.* (New York: Prentice Hall, 1994).

———. *Enemies of Intelligence: Knowledge & Power in American National Security.* (New York: Columbia University Press, 2007.

Bjorkman, James. *Fundamentalism, Revivalists and Violence in South Asia.* (San Francisco: Riverdale Co., 1988).

Boot, M. *The Savage Wars of Peace.* (New York, Basic Books, 2002).

Bowden, Mark. *Guests of the Ayatollah.* (New York: Atlantic Monthly Press, 2006).

Breckinridge, Scott. *The CIA and U.S. Intelligence System.* (Boulder: Westview Press, 1986).

Building Interreligious Trust in a Climate of Fear. U.S. Institute of Peace Special Report 99, February 2003.

Burns, J.F. and E. Eckholm. "In Western Iraq, Fundamentalists Hold U.S. at Bay," *The New York Times*, August 29, 2004.

Byman, Daniel, Kenneth Pollack and Gideon Rose. "The Rollback Fantasy," *Foreign Affairs*, January/February 1999, vol. 78, no. 1, pp. 24-41

Carr, Caleb. "William Pitt the Elder and the Avoidance of the American Revolution," in Robert Cowley (ed.), *What Ifs? Of American History.* (New York: G.F. Putnam's Sons, pp. 17-42).

"CIA Insider: The Threat We Refuse to Get," *The Washington Post*, July 11, 2004, p. B1.

Chubin, Shahram. *Iran's Nuclear Ambitions.* (New York: Carnegie Endowment for International Peace, 2006).

Cohn, Jonathan. "When Did Political Science Forget About Politics? Irrational Exuberance," *The New Republic* (New York), October 25, 1999, pp. 25-32.

Coll, Steve. *Ghost Wars: The Secret History of the CIA, Afghanistan and bin Laden, from the Soviet Invasion to September 10, 2001.* (New York: Penguin Books, 2004).

Cooley, John K. *Unholy Wars: Afghanistan, America and International Terrorism.* (Pluto Press, 2002).

Cooper, Helene. "Ahmadinejad, at Columbia, Parries and Puzzles," *The New York Times*, September 25, 2007, p. 1.

Cordesman, Anthony. H. *Iran's Developing Military Capabilities.* (Washington: The CSIS Press, 2005).

Crocker, Chester A. et. al. (eds.) *Herding Cats: Multiparty Mediation in a Complex World.* (Washington: U.S. Institute of Peace, 1999).

Danner, Mark. "Taking Stock of the Forever War, *The New York Times Magazine*, September 11, 2005, pp. 46-86.

Daugherty, William J. *Executive Secrets: Covert Action and the Presidency*. (Lexington, Univ. Press of Kentucky, 2004).

Defeating the Jihadists. A Century Foundation Task Force Report, The Century Foundation, 2005.

Dekmejian, R. H. *Spectrum of Terror*. (Washington: CQ Press, 2007).

Der Derian, James. *On Diplomacy*. (Cambridge, MA: Blackwell, 1987).

Diamond, Larry. *Squandered Victory*, (Henry Holt & Co., 2005).

Diamond, L. "What Went Wrong in Iraq." *Foreign Affairs*, September/ October 2004, pp. 34-56.

Dobbins, James, et al. *America's Role in Nation-Building: From Germany to Iraq*. (Santa Monica, CA: RAND, 2003).

Downs, Anthony. *Inside Bureaucracy*. (Boston, Little, Brown and Co., 1967).

Easterbrook, Gregg. "Science and God: A Warming Trend?" *SCIENCE*, vol. 277, August 13, 1997, pp. 890-93.

Esposito, John. *The Islamic Threat: Myth or Reality?* rev. ed. (Oxford, Oxford University Press, 1995).

Etzioni, Amitai. *From Empire to Community*. (New York: Palgrave Macmillan, 2006).

Falk, Richard. "The Religious Foundations of Humane Global Governance," unpublished paper prepared for Religion and World Order Symposium, Maryknoll, N.Y. May 1997.

Fallows, James. *Blind into Baghdad: America's War in Iraq*. (New York: Vintage Books, 2006.

———. "Blind into Baghdad," *The Atlantic*, vol. 293, no. 1, January-February, 2004, pp. 52-77.

———. "Will Iran be Next?" *The Atlantic*, December 2004, vol. 294, pp 97-111.

Ferguson, Charles D. and William C. Potter. *The Four Faces of Nuclear Terror*. (Monterey, CA: the Center for Nonproliferation Studies, 2004)

Fergusson, Niall. *Colossus: The Price of America's Empire.* (New York: The Penguin Press, 2004).

Fitzpatrick, Kathy R. "The Collapse of American Public Diplomacy: What diplomatic experts say about rebuilding America's image in the World—a view from the trenches" Unpublished paper from the 2008 International Studies Association Conference, San Francisco, CA.

Frankfurt, Harry G, *On Bullshit.* (Princeton, NJ: Princeton University Press, 2005).

Foreign Service Journal. focus issue on "An Uncertain Path Ahead: The Foreign Service as a Career," especially pp. 20-34.

Forging an Iran Strategy. American Foreign Policy Council (Wheaton, IL. August 15, 2006).

Friedman, Thomas L. *The Lexus and the Olive Tree.* (New York: Farrar Straus Giroux, 1999).

——. *The World is Flat.* (New York: Farrar Straus and Giroux, 2005).

Gearan, Ann. "U.S. Embassy Not Safe Enough," *Lexington Herald-Leader*, May 2, 2007, p. 3.

George, Alexander. *Bridging the Gap.* (Washington: U.S. Institute of Peace, 1998).

——. *On Foreign Policy.* (Boulder, CO: Paradigm Publishers, 2006).

Gingrich, Newt. "Rogue State Department," *Foreign Policy* (Washington), July/August 2003, p. 42.

Goodstein, Laurie. "Muslim Leaders Confront Terror Threat Within Islam," *The New York Times*, September 2, 2005.

Griffiths, Bede. *A New Vision of Reality: Western Science, Eastern Mysticism and Christian Faith.* (Springfield, IL: Templegate Press, 1989).

Grotius, Hugo and A.C. Campbell. *The Rights of War and Peace: Including the Law of Nature and Nations.* (New York: M.W. Dunne, 1901).

Guillemin, Jeanne. Biological Weapons. (New York: Columbia Univ. Press, 2005).

Haas, Richard N. *The Opportunity*. (Cambridge, MA: Perseus Books Group, 2005).

Harik, Judith Palmer. *Hezbollah: The Changing Face of Terrorism*. (New York: I.B. Tauris, 2004).

Harris, Sam. *The End of Faith*. (New York: W.W. Norton, 2005).

———. *Letter to a Christian Nation*. (New York: Alfred A. Knopf, 2006), pp. 87-91.

Harrop, William C. *"Major International Challenges the U.S. will Face in 2005,"* in the Internet journal, www.AmericanDiplomacy.org.

Hauptman, Emily. "From Opposition to Accommodation: How Rockefeller Foundation Grants Redefined Relations Between Political Theory and Social Science in the 1950s," *American Political Science Review* 100 (November 2006): pp. 643-49.

Hentz, J.J. *The Obligation of Empire: United States' Grand Strategy for a New Century*. (Lexington: University Press of Kentucky, 2004).

Herring, George M. *America's Longest War: The United States and Vietnam, 1950-1975*. (New York: McGraw Hill, 1996).

Herring, George M. and John C. Carroll. *Modern American Diplomacy*. (Wilmington, DE: Scholarly Resources Inc., 1996).

Hersh, Seymour. "Last Stand," *The New Yorker* (New York), July 10 2006, pp. 42-49.

———. "Preparing the Battlefield." The New Yorker (New York), July 7 & 14, pp. 61-67.

———. "The Stovepipe: How Conflicts between the Bush Administration and the intelligence community marred the reporting on Iraq's weapons," *The New Yorker*, October 27, 2003, pp. 7-87.

Hoffman, Bruce. *Inside Terrorism*. (New York: Columbia Univ. Press, 2006).

Holmes, James R. *Theodore Roosevelt and World Order*. (Washington: Potomac Books, 2006),

Hunter, F. Robert. *The Palestinian Uprising*. (University of California Press, 1991).

Iran: Time for a new Approach: Report of an Independent Task Force Sponsored by the Council on Foreign Relations. (New York: Council on Foreign Relations, 2004).

Janis, Irving L. *Groupthink: Psychological Studies of Policy Decisions and Fiascoes.* (New York: Houghton Mifflin Company, 1982).

Jeffreys-Jones Rohodri. *The CIA and American Democracy.* (New Haven Yale Univ. Press, 1989).

Jervis, Robert. *American Foreign Policy in a New Era.* (Routledge, NY: Routledge, 2005).

Joes, A. *America and Guerilla Warfare.* (Lexington: University Press of Kentucky, 2006).

———. *Resisting Rebellion.* (University Press of Kentucky, 2004).

Johnson, Chalmers. *Blowback: The Costs and Consequences of American Empire.* (New York: Henry Holt, 2000).

———. *The Sorrows of Empire: Militarism, Secrecy, and the End of the Republic.* (New York: Metropolitan Books, 2004).

Johnson, Loch. *America's Secret Power.* (Oxford: Oxford Univ. Press, 1989).

Johnson, Loch. (ed.) *Strategic Intelligence.* (five volumes) (New York: Praeger Security International, 2007).

Johnson, Loch and James J. Wirtz (eds.). *Strategic Intelligence: Windows into a Secret World.* (Los Angeles: Roxbury Publishing Co., 2004).

Johnstone, Douglas and Cynthia Sampson. *Religion: The Missing Dimension of Statecraft.* (Oxford: Oxford Univ. Press, 1994).

Jones, Jeremy. *Negotiating Change: The New Politics of the Middle East.* (I.B. Tauris, 2007).

Kaplan, Fred. *Daydream Believers.* (New York: John Wiley & Sons, 2008).

Kaplan, Robert D. *An Empire in the Wilderness.* (New York: Vintage Books, 1998).

Kaplan, Robert D. *Warrior Politics: Why Leadership Demands a Pagan Ethos.* (New York: Vintage Books, 2002).

Kean, Thomas H. and Lee Hamilton. "Intelligence Reform can not wait," *Louisville Courier-Journal*, September 12, 2004 p. H-1.

Kelsay, John. *Islam and War.* (Louisville, KY: Westminster/John Knox Press, 1993).

Kennedy, Paul. "Embassies for Sale," *The International Herald Tribune*, May 14, 2007, p. 1.

Kessler, Glenn. "Embassy Staff in Baghdad Inadequate," *The Washington Post*, June 19, 2007, p. A1

Khalidi, Rashid. *Resurrecting Empire: Western Footprints and America's Perilous Path in the Middle East.* (Boston: Beacon Press, 2005).

Kinser, Stephen. *All the Shah's Men.* (Hoboken: John Wiley & sons, 2003).

Kohut, Andrew and Bruce Stokes. *America Against the World.* (New York: Henry Holt and Company, 2006).

Krauthamer, Charles. "*The Unipolar Moment Revisited,*" *The National Interest*, Winter 2002/3, pp. 5-17.

Krugman, Paul. *The Great Unraveling: Loosing Our Way in the New Century.* (New York, W.W. Norton, 2005).

Langhorne, Richard. "New Emissaries and No Emissaries: The Representation of New Voices in Global Politics," unpublished paper for August 28-30, 2000 CISS/International Studies Association Conference, Washington, D.C.

Lewis, Bernard. *The Crisis of Islam: Holy War and Holy Terror.* (New York: The Modern Library, 2003).

_____.*What Went Wrong? Western Impact and Middle Eastern Response.* (Oxford, Oxford University Press, 2002).

Lewis, C.S. *Mere Christianity.* (New York: Macmillan, 1952).

Lewis, C.S. (writing as N. W. Clerk). *A Grief Observed.* (Greenwich: The Seabury Press, 1963).

Lewis Lapham. *Gag Rule: On the Suppression of Dissent and Stifling of Democracy.* (New York: Penguin, 2004).

Lind, Michael. *The American Way of Strategy.* (New York: Oxford Univ. Press, 2006).

Linsday, J.M. and I. H. Daalder. *America Unbound: The Bush Revolution in Foreign Policy.* (Washington: The Brookings Institution Press, 2003).

MacFarquhar, Neil, "How Iran's Leader Keeps the West off Balance," *The New York Times*, December 13, p. wk 5.

Magstadt, T. M. *An Empire If You Can Keep It.* (Washington: CQ Press, 2003).

Martin, William. "The Christian Right and American Foreign Policy," *Foreign Policy*, spring 1999, pp. 66-81.

Mazur, Jay. "Labor's new Internationalism," *Foreign Affairs*, January/February 2000, vol. 79, no. 1, pp. 79-93.

McDougall, Walter A. "Religion in Diplomatic History," in *American Diplomacy*, an Internet magazine found at: www.unc.edu/depts/diplomat/amdipl_12/mcdougall_rel.html

Mead, Walter Russell. *"America's Sticky Power,"* *Foreign Policy*, March/April 2004, pp. 46-53.

———. "God's Country?" *Foreign Affairs*, September/October 2006, vol. 85, no. 5, pp. 24-43.

———. *Power, Terror, Peace and War: America's Grand Strategy in a World at Risk.* (New York: Knopf, 2004).

———. *Special Providence: American Foreign Policy and How it Shaped the World.* (Alfred A. Knopf, New York, 2001).

Mearsheimer, John and Stephen Walt, "Iraq: An Unnecessary War," *Foreign Policy*, January/February 2003, pp. 50-59.

Merry, Robert W. *Sands of Empire.* (New York: Simon & Schuster, 2005).

Mingst, Karen. *Essentials of International Relations.* (New York: W.W. Norton and Company, 2004).

Murphy, Cullen. *Are We Rome? The Fall of an Empire and the Fate of America.* (New York: Houghton Mifflin Co., 2007).

Murphy, Dan. "U.S. hawks see strikes on Iran as less likely now," *The Christian Science Monitor*, March 18, 2007.

Murray, W. and R. J. Scales Jr. *The Iraq War.* (Cambridge: The Belknap Press of Harvard University Press, 2003).

Nagel, John A. (ed.). *U.S. Army Field/Marine Corps Counterinsurgency Manual.* (Washington: U.S. government Printing Office, 2007).

Nasr, Vali. *The Shia Revival: How Conflicts within Islam Will Shape the Future.* (New York, W.W. Norton, 2006).

Naylor, Sean. *Not a Good Day to Die.* (New York: Berkley Books, 2005).

Newsom, David D. *Diplomacy and American Democracy.* (Bloomington: Indiana University Press, 1988).

Niebuhr, Reinhold. *Christian Realism and Political Problems.* (New York: Charlies Scribner's Sons, 1953).

———. *The Irony of American History.* (New York: Charles Scribner's Sons, 1952).

———. *Moral Man and Immoral Society.* (New York: Charles Scribner's Sons, 1932).

Nye, J. S. Jr. *The Paradox of American Power.* (New York: Oxford University Press, 2002).

———. *Soft Power.* (New York: Public Affairs Press, 2004).

Odom, William E. *Fixing Intelligence.* (New Haven: Yale Univ. Press, 2006).

Odom, William and Richard Dujarric. *America's Inadvertant Empire.* (New Haven: Yale Nota Bene, 2005).

ORBIS. Special Issue on Religion, Spring 1998, vol. 42, no. 2.

Oren, Michael B. Power. *Fantasy and Faith: America in the Middle East, 1776 to the Present.* (W. W. Norton & Co, 2007).

OxfordAnalytica. http://www.forbes.com/2007/08/22/bush-anti-americanism-cx_0823oxfordanalytica_print.html.

Peterson, P. "Riding for a Fall," *Foreign Affairs*, September/October 2004, pp. 111-115.

Pieratt-Seeley, Carey. "The Development of the Public Sphere Within the Protestant Church in the German Democratic Republic, 1950-89," paper presented at the International Studies Association Southern Regional meeting, Lexington, KY, November 12-14, 1999.

Pilar, Paul. *Terrorism and U.S. Foreign Policy*. (Brookings Institution Press, Washington, 2001).

Pilon, Juliana Geran. *Why America is Such a Hard Sell: Beyond Pride and Prejudice*. (Rowman & Littlefield, New York, 2007).

Pollack, Kenneth M. *The Persian Puzzle: The Conflict between Iran and America*. (New York: Random House, 2004).

Pollack, Kenneth M. "Spies, Lies, and Weapons: What Went Wrong," *The Atlantic*, vol. 293, no. 1, January-February 2004, pp. 78-92.

Porter, Robert Odawi. "Question 2: What Kind of Shared Citizenship is Actually Possible in a World of Separate Nation-States? Two Rows, Two Peoples, Two Nations: The Meaning of Haudenosaunee Citizenship," *International Studies Review* 3 (September 2005), pp. 512-15.

Priest, Dana. *The Mission*. (W.W. North & Co., 2003).

Ramsey, Paul. *The Just War: Force and Political Responsibility*. (Boulder, CO: Rowman & Littlefield Publishers, 1983).

Randal, Jonathan. *Osama: The Making of a Terrorist*. (New York: Alfred A. Knopf, 2004).

Rashid, Ahmed. *Taliban: Militant Islam, Oil and Fundamentalism in Central Asia*. (Yale University Press, 2000),

Rasmussen, Larry (ed.). *Reinhold Niebuhr: Theologian of Public Life*. (Fortress Press, 1991).

Ribuffe, Leo. "Religion and American Foreign Policy: The Story of a Complex Relationship," *National Interest*, Summer 1998, no. 52, pp. 37-50.

Richardson, Elliot. *Reflections of a Radical Moderate.* (New York, Pantheon Books, 1996).

Richelson, Jeffery T. *The U.S. Intelligence Community.* (Boulder: Westview, 1995).

Risen, James. *State Of War: The Secret History of the CIA and the Bush Administration.* (New York: Free Press, 2006).

Roosevelt, Kim, *Countercoup: The Struggle for Control of Iran.* (New York: McGraw-Hill, 1979).

Rothkopf, David J. *Running the World: The Inside Story of the National Security Council and the architects of America's Power.* (New York: Public Affairs Press, 2005).

Rubin, Barry (ed.). *The Politics of Terrorism.* (Baltimore: Johns Hopkins Foreign Policy Institute, 1989).

Saunders, Harold. *Politics is About Relationships.* (New York: Palgrave Macmillan, 2005).

Schriver. Donald. *An Ethic for Enemies: Forgiveness in Politics.* (New York: Oxford University Press, 1995).

Selliktar, Ofira. *Failing the Crystal Ball Test.* (Westport: Praeger, 2000).

Selliktar, Ofira. *The Politics of Intelligence and American Wars with Iraq.* (New York: Palgrave Macmillan, 2008).

Sick, Garry. *All Fall Down.* (London: I. B. Tauris, 1985).

Slavin, Barbara. *Bitter Friends, Bosom Enemies.* (New York: St. Martin's Press, 2007).

Smith, Rupert. *The Utility of Force: The Art of War in the Modern World.* (New York: Knopf, 2007).

Soderberg, Nancy. The *Superpower Myth: The Use and Misuse of American Might.* (New York: John Wiley and Sons, 2005).

Spalding, E. E. *The First Cold Warrior: Harry Truman, Containment, and the Remaking of Liberal Internationalism.* (Lexington: University Press of Kentucky, 2006).

Stassen, Glen. *Just Peacemaking: Ten Practices for Abolishing War.* (Cleveland, OH: The Pilgrim Press, 1998).

Stempel, John D. *Inside the Iranian Revolution*. (Bloomington: Indiana University Press, 1981).

Stempel, John D. "Religion and Diplomacy," *Lexington Theological Quarterly*, vol. 40, no. 3, Fall 2005. pp. 153-72.

Stempel, John D. "Religion, Politics and Terrorism," *Lexington Theological Quarterly*, vol. 40, no. 3, Fall 2005, pp. 173-189.

Sternberg, Robert J. *Why Smart People Can Be So Stupid*. (New Haven, CT: Yale University Press, 2002).

Summers, L.H. "*America Overdrawn*," *Foreign Policy*, July/August 2004, pp. 46-49.

Suskind, Ron. *The One Percent Doctrine*. (New York: Simon and Schuster, 2006).

Takeyh, Ray. *Hidden Iran: Paradox and Power in the Islamic Republic*. (New York: Times Books, 2006).

Tenet, George. *At the Center of the Storm*. (New York: HarperCollins, 2007).

Todd, E. *After the Empire*. (New York, Columbia University Press, 2001).

Tuchman, Barbara. *March of Folly*. (New York; Ballantine Books, 1984).

Tucker, R. W. and D. C. Hendrickson. "The Sources of American Legitimacy," *Foreign Affairs*, November/December 2004, vol. 83, no. 6.

U.S. Department of State, Transcript of Secretary of State Condoleezza Rice's remarks in the East Auditorium, Department of State, Washington, D.C., 2007.

"U.S. Envoy on Faith Not Welcome," Pioneer News Service, New Delhi, September 13, 1999.

Walt, Stephen M. "Rigor or Rigor Mortis? Rational Choice and Security Studies," *International Security 23* (Spring 1999), pp. 5-48.

———. *Taming American Power*. (New York: Norton, 2006).

Weigel, George. *Just War and the Gulf War*. (Washington: Ethics and Public Policy Center, 1991).

Wright, Robin. *Dreams and Shadows: The Future of the Middle East.* (New York: The Penguin Press, 2008).

———. "Stress Taking Toll on Foreign Service," *The Washington Post*, June 20, 2007, p. A17.

———. *The Last Great Revolution: Turmoil and Transformation in Iran.* (New York: Alfred A. Knopf, 2000).

Woodward, Bob. *Plan of Attack.* (New York: Simon & Schuster, 2004).

———. *State of Denial.* (New York: Simon & Schuster, 2006).

Wuthnow, Robert. "Understanding Religion and Politics," *Daedalus*, Summer 1991, pp. 1-20.

Zakaria, Fareed. "What Iranians Least Expect," *Newsweek*, October 20, 2006.

Zinni, Anthony. Center for Defense Information, "Eye on Iraq," May 22, 2004 and "They've Screwed Up," http://www.cbsnews.com/stories/2004/04/21/60minutes/printable618896.shtml

APPENDIX A

Seven books to significantly increase your understanding of international relations and foreign policy.

Odom, William and Richard Dujarric. *America's Inadvertent Empire.* (New Haven: Yale Nota Bene, 2005). The best description of where America is with respect to the world.

Merry, Robert W. *Sands of Empire.* (New York: Simon & Schuster, 2005). Excellent and very readable history of how U.S. Foreign Policy has evolved over the past sixty years.

Saunders, Harold. *Politics is About Relationships.* (New York: Palgrave Macmillan, 2005). Detailed description of the goals and techniques of politics and diplomacy, by a master of the craft.

Smith, Rupert. *The Utility of Force: The Art of War in the Modern World.* (New York: Knopf, 2007). The most insightful current book about contemporary military affairs and issues by a veteran British general.

Tuchman, Barbara. *March of Folly.* (New York; Ballantine Books, 1984). A selected multi-century look at major mistakes and follies.

Khalidi, Rashid. *Resurrecting Empire: Western Footprints and America's Perilous Path in the Middle East.* (Boston: Beacon Press, 2005). The best, clearest and most concise explanation of how America got where it is in the Middle East.

Hoffman, Bruce. *Inside Terrorism.* (New York: Columbia Univ. Press, 2006). An excellent objective guide to world terrorism without boogeyman comments.

Each year the faculty of the University of Kentucky selects eight-ten books for our students to read over the summer. You can update your reading each year in May.

The current list can be found on the internet at:

http://www.pattersonschool.uky.edu then click on "summer reading" under "resources" in left-hand column.

APPENDIX B

www.fpa.org .... Foreign Policy Association

www.state.gov .... U.S. State Department

usinfo.state.gov .... U.S. information service

www.intelligence.gov .... U.S. Intelligence Community

www.cfr.org .... New York Council of Foreign Relations

www.afsaorg/publications .... U.S. Foreign Service Association

www.embassyworld.com/embassy/directory .... List of
Embassies worldwide

www.un.org .... United Nations

www.un.org/databases .... UN databases

www.nato.org .... North Atlantic Treaty Organization

www.terrorism.com .... Terrorist information

www.isanet.org .... International Studies Association

www.oas.org .... Organization of American States

www.iaea.org .... International Atomic Energy Agency

www. opew.org .... Chemical weapons www.carnegieendowment.org..Security policy

www.unhcr.ch .... UN Refugee Organization

www.undp.org...UN Development Program

www.worldwatch.org......................................Environmental organization

www.ito.org .... International Trade Organization

www.icrd.org/projects.html................. International Center for Religion
and Diplomacy

www.juancole.com/ .... Major Middle East comment site

GLOSSARY

Abu Ghraib—An Iraqi prison made famous by brutal U.S. interrogation of suspected Iraqi militants.

Bader-Meinhof Gang—Particularly violent German radical group of the 1970s, now defunct.

Ball, George—Undersecretary of State under Dean Rusk in 1960s opposed deeper involvement in Vietnam.

Battle of the Bulge—Attempted breakthrough of German forces in 1944 against allied armies which failed.

Boot, Max—Neoconservative writer who favors U.S. interventions abroad.

Bremer, Paul—Head of the Iraq Provisional Coalition Authority, 2004-2005.

Burke, Edmund—18th century British Tory politician and conservative thinker, favored American independence over military repression.

China: Status of Taiwan and revaluation of Chinese Yuan—two political/economic issues on which the U.S. and China differ significantly enough to raise the prospect of violence between them.

Coalition Provisional Authority—The U.S. ruling authority in Iraq, 2004-5.

Cold War—The state of tension that existed between the U.S. and the Soviet Union from 1947-89.

Committee on Public Information–George Creel—U.S. propaganda agency in World War I and its leader

Davis, Vince—Defense scholar and a major developer of the 1987 Gold-Water-Nichols legislation to reform U.S. Joint Chiefs of State. Also director of University of Kentucky's Patterson School, 1971-93.

Donne, John—19th century English writer who stressed unity of man kind.

Donovan, William O.—World War II founder head of the OSS in World War II.

Fall of the Berlin Wall—The collapse of East Germany in November 1989, triggered the destruction of the wall by the euphoric public. The wall separated West Berlin from East Berlin and the rest of East Germany and was considered a symbol of the Iron Curtain.

Feith, Douglas— Undersecretary of Defense, 3rd ranking official in U.S. Defense Department, 2001-2006. In charge of rebuilding Iraq, is credited with most major blunders in planning.

Francis Fukyama's democratic triumphalism—Name given to the collapse of the Soviet Union and the subsequent dominance of the western alliance..

Fundamentalist form of Islamic ideology—A system of Islamic thought.

Fundamentalist Islamic terrorism—Islamic movement which defines itself by a duty and willingness to kill for and die for their group. It is religious terrorism by those whose motivations are rooted in their interpretations of Islam.

Gandhi—Leader of 20th century Indian independent movement, noted for his non-violent resistance movement.

Germain, Lord George—18th century British Statesman and Secretary of State in North's government during American independence struggle, which he firmly opposed.

Global hegemon—A world dominant power. A title often assigned to the U.S.

Great White Fleet—U.S. Fleet of 16 Battleships which President Theodore Roosevelt sent around the world in 1907-1909.

Griffiths, Father Bede—20th century cross-cultural Catholic theologian who sketched out a "perennial philosophy" which reflected world religions' consensus on moral questions.

Grotius, Hugo—17th century Dutch Scholar who codified international practice into international law.

Guantanamo holding facility—A facility located at the Guantanamo Bay Naval Base where prisoners captured in Afghanistan after 9/11 are held.

Harris, Sam—Noted atheist writer.

Hegemony—A concept that is used to describe and explain the dominance of one social group over another, like a ruling group with dominance over others.

Hindu-Muslim conflicts—conflicts between religious groups, especially in India.

Hyperpower—Hyperpower or superpower is a term to describe a state or country that is militarily, economically, and technologically dominant on the world stage.

International actors—States, individuals, groups and international organizations.

Interventionist Policy—A policy of intervening in an other country's affairs to protect your own interests

Iranian Revolution—Replaced the Shah of Iran in February 1979 with control by Iranian religious leader led by Ayatollah Khomeini.

Islamic Jihadist—A person who opposes other faiths by force and violence.

Islamic Renaissance—Growing efforts by Islamic peoples to strengthen their place in the world.

Isolationist Era—The time from 1920-1941 when America turned away from active world involvement.

Janis, Irving—Author of seminal book, *Groupthink.*

Judeo-Christian tradition—religious heritage of Western Europe.

"Just War" doctrine—Defines what it is just to fight for.

Krauthamer, Charles —Neoconservative writer who coined the phrase "Unipolar moment."

Kristol, William—Neoconservative writer and editor of the National Standard.

Kyoto Treaty—The Kyoto Protocol is a protocol to the international Framework Convention on Climate Change with the objective of reducing greenhouse gases that cause climate change and 182 parties not including the U.S. have ratified the protocol.

Lewis, C. S.—English theologian and writer, 1898-1963.

Manifest Destiny—19th Century doctrine that said the U.S. has the right and destiny to conquer and civilize the North American Continent.

Marshall Plan—An American aid plan which saved Europe from collapse in 1948-55 by giving $13.5 billion in assistance.

Martin, Abe (Kin Hubbard)—Fictional character and purveyor of common sense in his newspaper column, 1930-70.

Multi-power imperial world post-World War I—France, Germany, Britain, Austria-Hungary, Russia and the United States.

Nasr, Vali—Islamic Scholar at New York Council of Foreign Relations.

Neoconservatives (also NeoCon)—Individuals who believe the U.S. should use U.S. military power unilaterally regardless of what allies or enemies think.

North, Frederick Lord—18th century British statesman and Prime Minister during much of the American revolution. Firmly against American independence.

Office of Strategic Services (ROSS)—World War II wartime U.S. intelligence agency, precursor of CIA

Palestinian radicals—Those Palestinians who refuse to consider a peace agreement with Israel.

Pearle, Richard—Neoconservative writer, sometime-government appointee. Very pugnacious.

Perennial Philosophy—Basic philosophical principals agreed upon by almost all major religions.

Philippines in 1899 (bloody war)—The civil war that broke out in the Philippines after the U.S. took over in 1898. Active fighting ended in 1903, while guerilla resistance continued until 1919.

Pax Americana—The peace brought by American power in the late 2oth century.

Realpolitik—The doctrine of "might" versus "right" in international affairs.

Red Brigades—European radical groups in the 1970s committed to violence and kidnapping.

Richelieu, Cardinal —17th century French foreign minister who also held ecclesiastical office.

Roosevelt, Franklin–"Good Neighbor" policy—A policy of U.S. collaboration with Latin America which replaced a decade-long interventionist policy in the 1930s

Secularization—Turn away from religion in modern societies.

Shah of Iran—Mohammad Reza Pahlavi, ruler of Iran from 1941 until overthrown by clerics led by Ayatollah Khomeini in 1979.

Shia Revival—Greater contemporary interest in and support of the Shia sect within Islam.

Shiites—Those Moslems who share faith in the return of the 12th Imam.

"Shock and Awe"—The sudden and overwhelming power used by U.S. forces in the invasion of Iraq in 2003 designed to paralyze the Iraq forces and destroy their will to fight.

Stassen, Glen—Prominent contemporary theologian who modernized doctrine of "Just Peace."

Sunnis—Majority sect in Islam, outnumber Shias about 4-1.

Taliban—A radical Muslim group in Afghanistan created by the U.S. and Pashtuns to fight the Russian invasion of Afghanistan.

Tora Bora—Name of the battle where Osama bin Laden and key leaders were able to escape allied forces in December 2001.

Treaty of Westphalia—Signed in 1648, decree that people would abide by their ruler's religion, which led to the creation of modern Diplomacy.

U.S. Central Command (CENTCOM)—One of five world-wide U.S. military commands. It includes the Middle East.

U.S.-Soviet bipolar era—1947-1989, when the U.S. and the Soviet Union dominated world affairs

Unilateralist—To do things without taking into account the views of others.

"Unipolar Moment"—Phrase used to describe the world briefly after the collapse of the Soviet Union.

Vienna Convention—International rules regulating diplomatic services created in 1815, revised 1961.

Vladimir Putin—Former Russian KGB officer, who became Russia's President, 2000-2008.

Zinni, General Tony—U.S. Central Command Commander in the late 1990s and severe critics of U.S. operations in lraq.

Zionism—Belief in the necessity for creation of the state of Israel and its expansion.

MAPS

AFGHANISTAN

ALGERIA

ARMENIA

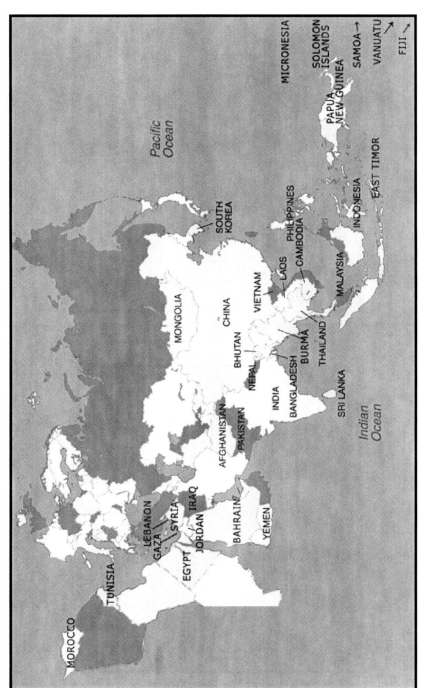

ASIA

AZERBAIJAN

BOSNIA HERZEGOVINA

BURMA

CHILE

FRANCE

GERMANY

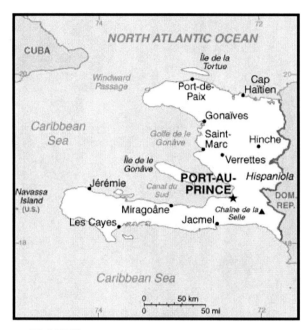

HAITI

INDONESIA

IRELAND

JAPAN

KAZAKHSTAN

KOSOVO

KUWAIT

LEBANON

LATIN AMERICA

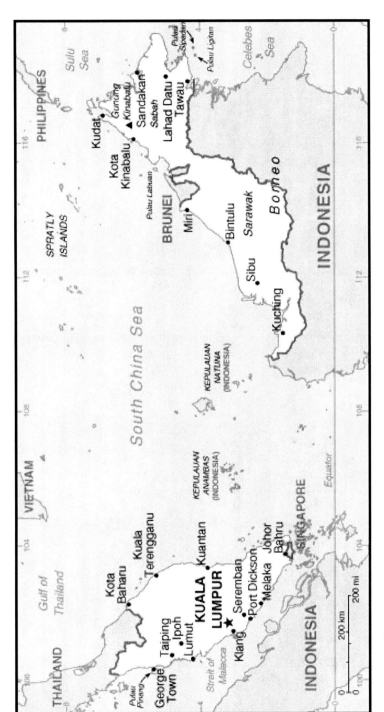

MALAYSIA

PHILIPPINES

POLAND

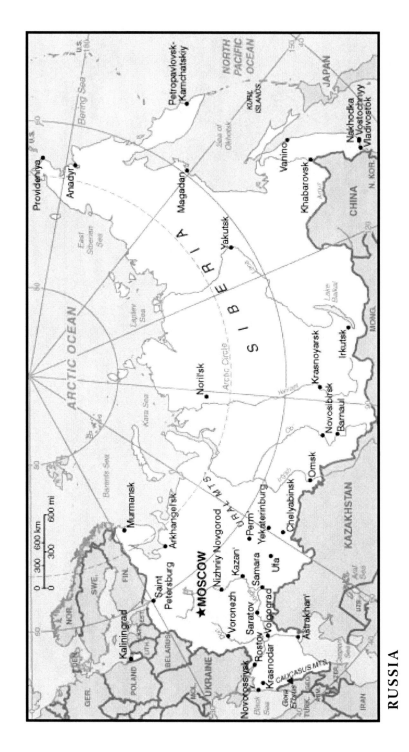

RUSSIA

RWANDA

SERBIA

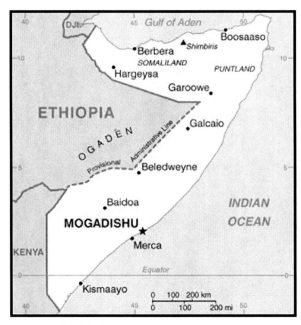

SOMALIA

SOUTH KOREA

SPAIN

SRI LANKA

SUDAN

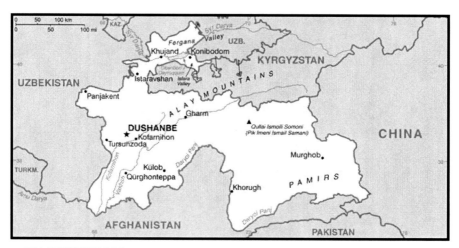

TAJIKISTAN

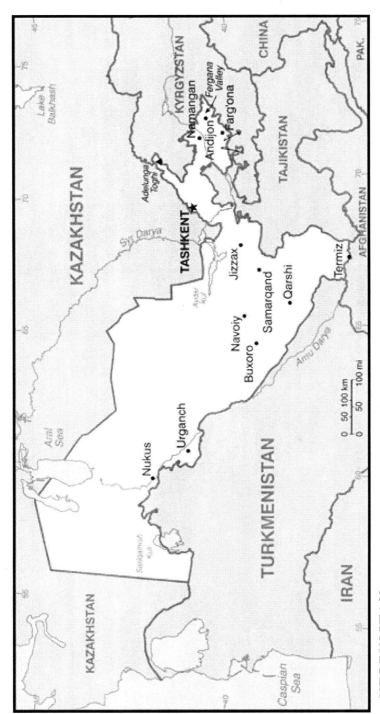

UZBEKISTAN

MAP INDEX

All maps courtesy of The University of Texas Libraries, The University of Texas at Austin, unless otherwise noted.

INDEX

Printed in the United States
125919LV00003B/112-249/P